Bluegrass Banjo Method
Book One

by

Jack Hatfield

Fifth Edition, August 1998
© Copyright 1989 Hatfield Music
© Original Copyright 1979 as "Scruggs Style Banjo Method"
All rights reserved

Compact Disc Program Index

1	Tuning the Banjo	37	Lesson 13 - The Reverse Roll
2	Lesson 1 - The Alternating Thumb Roll	38	MOUNTAIN DEW, Slow
3	Exercise 1	39	MOUNTAIN DEW, Accompanied
4	GOOD NIGHT LADIES - PART ONE, Slow	40	Lesson 14 - The Hammer-On
5	Lesson 2 - Two Simple Chords, Exercise 2	41	BURY ME BENEATH THE WILLOW, Slow
6	Exercise 3	42	BURY ME BENEATH THE WILLOW, Accompanied
7	GOOD NIGHT LADIES - PART TWO, Slow	43	Lesson 15 - The Pull - Off, Pull-Off Exercises
8	GOOD NIGHT LADIES, Accompanied	44	CRIPPLE CREEK, Slow
9	Lesson 3 - The Forward , Roll	45	CRIPPLE CREEK, Accompanied
10	BOIL THEM CABBAGE, Slow	46	Lesson 16 - The Reverse Roll #2
11	BOIL THEM CABBAGE, Accompanied	47	The Tag Lick
12	Lesson 4 - Changing Strings With Forward Roll, Ex. 4	48	OLD TIME RELIGION, Slow
13	TOM DOOLEY, Slow	49	OLD TIME RELIGION, Accompanied
14	TOM DOOLEY, Accompanied	50	Lesson 17 - The Foggy Mountain Roll, Foggy Mt. Lick
15	Lesson 5 - Counting Time, Exercise 5	51	TRAIN '45, Slow
16	Lesson 6 - The Pinch, Exercise 6	52	TRAIN '45, Accompanied
17	SOURWOOD MOUNTAIN, Slow	53	Lesson 18 - The Alternating Middle Roll
18	SOURWOOD MOUNTAIN, Accompanied	54	OLD JOE CLARK, Slow
19	Lesson 7 - Pickup Notes, Exercise 7	55	OLD JOE CLARK, Accompanied
20	TWO DOLLAR BILL, Slow	56	Lesson 19 - The Backward Roll
21	TWO DOLLAR BILL, Accompanied	57	HANDSOME MOLLY, Slow
22	Lesson 8 - Forward Roll #2	58	HANDSOME MOLLY, Accompanied
23	Exercise 8	59	Lesson 20 - The Backward-Forward Roll
24	MY OLD KENTUCKY HOME - VERSE, Slow	60	JOHN HENRY, Slow
25	Lesson 9 - A Simple Ending Lick	61	JOHN HENRY, Accompanied
26	Exercise 9	62	Lesson 21 - The D Chord, WILL THE CIRCLE BE UNBROKEN
27	MY OLD KENTUCKY HOME - CHORUS, Slow	63	Lesson 22 - Another D Formation, D BANJO BOOGIE
28	MY OLD KENTUCKY HOME, Accompanied	64	Lesson 23 - The Em and Am Chords, SAIL AWAY LADIES
29	Lesson 10 - Double Endings, HOME SWEET HOME	65	Lesson 24 - The F Chord, LITTLE MAGGIE
30	HOME SWEET HOME, Accompanied	66	Lesson 25 - The A, B7 Chords, MAKE ME A PALLET...FLOOR
31	Lesson 11 - The Slide, Slide Exercises	67	Chord - Roll Exercises
32	COMING 'ROUND THE MOUNTAIN, Slow	68	Endings
33	COMING 'ROUND THE MOUNTAIN, Accompanied	69	WHOA MULE, WHOA
34	Lesson 12 - Two-Measure Rolls	70	JOHN HARDY
35	BANKS OF THE OHIO, Slow	71	DOWN YONDER
36	BANKS OF THE OHIO, Accompanied	72	ROCKY TOP

The author with Earl Scruggs, the "Father of Bluegrass Banjo"

TABLE OF CONTENTS

About the Author 6

Foreward 7

Parts of the Banjo 8

Tuning the Banjo 9

Holding the Banjo 11

The Picks 12

Right-Hand Position 14

Reading Tablature 16

BOOK ONE: Basic Rolls and Left-Hand Techniques

Lesson 1 The Roll 19
           Melody Notes and Fill Notes 20
           Exercise 1 21
           Left-Hand Position 22
           GOOD NIGHT LADIES - Part One 23

Lesson 2 Two Simple Chords 24
           Exercise 2 25
           Exercise 3 26
           GOOD NIGHT LADIES - Part Two 27

Lesson 3 The Forward Roll 28
           BOIL THEM CABBAGE 28

Lesson 4 Changing Strings with the Forward Roll . . . 29
           Exercise 4 29
           TOM DOOLEY 30

Lesson 5 Counting Time 31
           Exercise 5 33

Lesson 6	The Pinch	34
	Exercise 6	35
	SOURWOOD MOUNTAIN	36
Lesson 7	Pick-up Notes	37
	Exercise 7	38
	TWO DOLLAR BILL	39
Lesson 8	Forward Roll #2	40
	Assigning Left-Hand Fingers	40
	Exercise 8	41
	MY OLD KENTUCKY HOME (Verse)	42
Lesson 9	A Simple Ending Lick	43
	Exercise 9	44
	MY OLD KENTUCKY HOME (Chorus)	45
	Practicing Effectively	46
Lesson 10	Repeat Marks and Double Endings	48
	HOME SWEET HOME	49
Lesson 11	The Slide	50
	COMING 'ROUND THE MOUNTAIN	51
Lesson 12	Two-Measure Rolls	52
	BANKS OF THE OHIO	53
Lesson 13	The Reverse Roll	54
	MOUNTAIN DEW	55
Lesson 14	The Hammer-On	56
	BURY ME BENEATH THE WILLOW	57
Lesson 15	The Pull-Off	58
	CRIPPLE CREEK	60
Lesson 16	The Reverse Roll #2	61
	The Tag Lick	62
	OLD TIME RELIGION	63
Lesson 17	The Foggy Mountain Roll	64
	TRAIN '45	65
Lesson 18	The Alternating Middle Roll	66
	OLD JOE CLARK	66

Lesson 19	The Backward Roll	67
	HANDSOME MOLLY	67
Lesson 20	The Backward-Forward Roll	68
	JOHN HENRY	69
	Basic Chord Formations	70
	Playing with a Rhythm Guitarist	70
Lesson 21	The **D** Chord	71
	WILL THE CIRCLE BE UNBROKEN	71
Lesson 22	Another **D** Formation	72
	D BANJO BOOGIE	72
Lesson 23	The **E** minor and **A** minor Chords	73
	SAIL AWAY LADIES	73
Lesson 24	The **F** Chord	74
	LITTLE MAGGIE	74
Lesson 25	The **A** and **B⁷** Chords	75
	MAKE ME A PALLET ON YOUR FLOOR	75

Chord-Roll Exercises 76

The Rest 78

Endings 79

SONG SECTION

WHOA MULE, WHOA 84

JOHN HARDY 85

DOWN YONDER 86

ROCKY TOP 88

Index of Songs 91

ABOUT THE AUTHOR

Jack Hatfield has been a professional banjo instructor for twenty-five years at the time of this printing and has taught thousands to play the five-string banjo using this book. He is best known for his contributions to *Banjo Newsletter*, the foremost source of banjo information in the world. His early *Scruggs Corner* columns in this magazine analyzed the style of Earl Scruggs, the "father of bluegrass banjo". Jack then authored the *Beginner's Corner* column for several years, and is currently writing a column for more advanced banjoists called *Concepts and Systems*. He also writes articles, reviews and interviews for Banjo Newsletter. Jack is also director of banjo newsletter workshops, seminars held all over the U.S.A. featuring top artists, craftsmen, and BNL contributors.

Jack entertains at tourist venues such as *Dollywood* theme park and the *Dixie Stampede* in Pigeon Forge, TN. He is banjoist and band leader for *True Blue,* a bluegrass band which is very active on the convention circuit. He has worked with internationally acclaimed mandolinist Red Rector, guitar champion Steve Kaufman, Ava Barber and Dick Dale from the *Lawrence Welk* TV show, and has served as band leader for Freida Parton, Dolly' sister. He was a featured instrumentalist on the *Saturday Night Barndance*, a live radio show heard in over 20 states on WNOX, 990 AM, Knoxville, TN. Jack has also been a finalist in the *National Banjo Championship* at Winfield, Kansas. He publishes books and play-along recordings for banjo, mandolin, guitar, and fiddle and publishes books for all four of these instruments, including several titles for *Mel Bay Publications, Inc.*, the world's largest publisher of stringed instrument instructional materials. He also markets his instructional materials and accessories for banjo players via his mail order business, *Hatfield Music.*

FOREWARD

This book is designed to teach the beginner the basics of three-finger Scruggs style banjo technique. It is a carefully graduated step-by-step guide which can be understood by those having no previous experience with the banjo or with music of any sort.

The most popular techniques are labeled, categorized, and arranged to give the student a solid foundation upon which he can build his own style.

This method is designed for group, individual, or self instruction. The songs were carefully selected for their familiarity among beginners, adaptability to three-finger style banjo, and their popularity among bluegrass players.

DEDICATION

This edition of <u>Bluegrass Banjo Method</u> - Book One, is dedicated to the memory of Hub Nitchie, who helped countless banjo players (including me) in their development.

Jack Hatfield
JH

PARTS OF THE BANJO

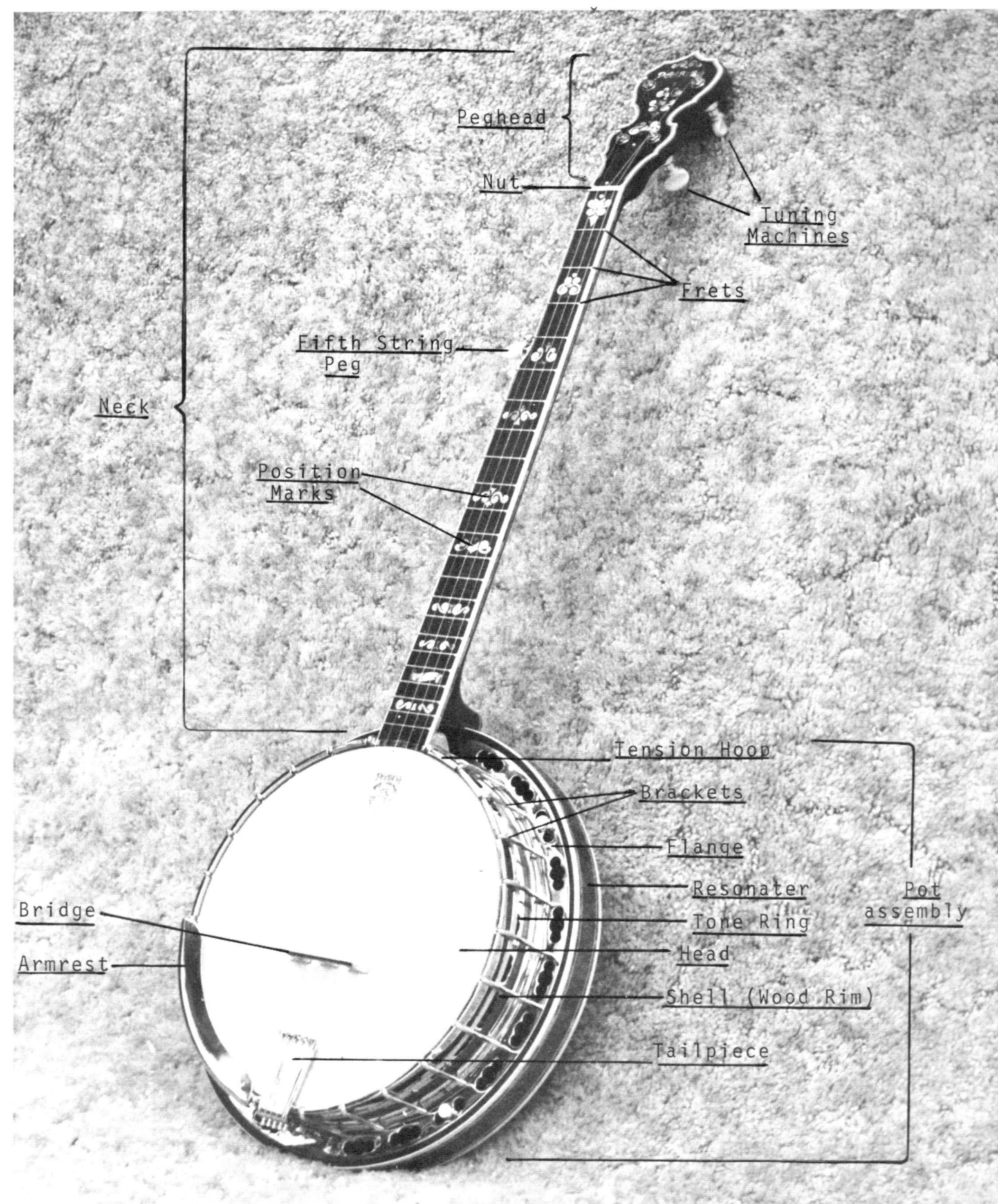

TUNING THE BANJO

The banjo can be tuned to any other instrument which is already in tune. If using a piano, tune the first string (**D**) to the **D** above middle C.

First String	- **D'**
Second String	- **B**
Third String	- **G**
Fourth String	- **D**
Fifth String	- **G'**

This will tune the banjo to *Standard* or *Concert* pitch. A tuning fork or banjo pitch pipe can also help in tuning to standard pitch.

It is not always necessary to be tuned to standard pitch if playing unaccompanied. The banjo must, however, be in tune with itself. Here is a procedure which allows you tune the banjo to itself when another instrument or tuning device is unavailable.

1. Play the fifth string *open* (without fretting it). This note will be used as a reference note to which the other strings will then be tuned.

2. Play the first (bottom) string while holding it down behind the fifth fret. It should sound the same as the fifth string played open. If it is higher or lower in pitch, adjust it by turning the tuning peg. Keep doing this until the two notes are exactly the same pitch.

3. Now that the first string is in tune, it will be used to tune the second string. Play the first string open, then play the second string while holding it down behind the third fret. Proceed as before until the two strings sound exactly the same.

4. To tune the third string, play the third string at the fourth fret. Adjust the tuning peg until it sounds the same as the second string played open.

5. The fourth string noted at the fifth fret should sound the same as the third string played open.

The banjo should now be reasonably in tune. However, sometimes the whole process may have to be repeated two or three times to fine-tune the banjo. Here is a summary of the previously described procedure:

Fifth String Open = First String, Fifth Fret
First String Open = Second String, Third Fret
Second String Open = Third String, Fourth Fret
Third String Open = Fourth String, Fifth Fret

There are other factors to consider in order to insure that the banjo stays in tune for a reasonable length of time. Be sure the strings are kept clean and are changed after every 25 to 30 hours of playing time. Be sure that the bridge is in its proper location and that the neck is straight. Check to see that the neck is fastened tightly to the pot assembly and that the head is tight and in good condition. The adjusting screw on friction-type tuners should be kept tight enough so that it will not slip, but not so tight as to strip the threads. Any worn tuners should be replaced. Geared tuners are best, including the fifth string tuner.

Any reputable stringed instrument dealer can inspect your banjo at little or no cost and repair any parts that are worn or broken.

HOLDING THE BANJO

It is easiest to learn to play while in a sitting position. Sit with your back straight and both feet on the floor. The use of a banjo strap is recommended. The extra support from the use of the strap will give the left hand more freedom. If standing up is preferred, adjust the strap so that the banjo is held at the same level as when sitting. In other words, your elbows and wrists should be bent at the same angle whether sitting or standing.

THE PICKS

Picks are used to insure that a banjo player gets adequate volume and consistent tone from all strings. The fingerpicks are placed on the index and middle fingers of the right hand. The extended portion of the pick should be against the inside of the finger, not against the fingernail. The picks can be shaped to fit the fingers using needle nose pliers. The flat area should be rounded out to prevent the pick from cutting into the finger. The part that touches the strings should be curved, the tip of the fingerpick being very close to the fingernail.

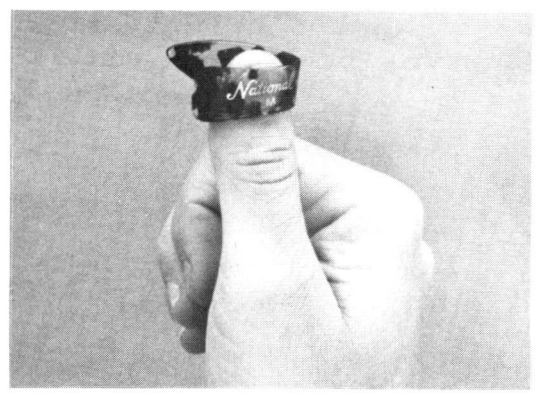
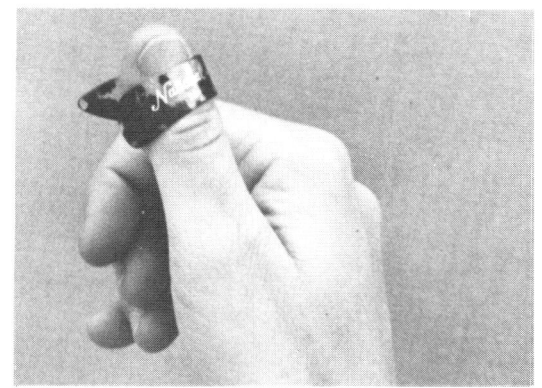

Incorrect   Correct

The thumbpick should be worn with the part that touches the string pointing toward the banjo. It, too, should be shaped to fit comfortably. Plastic picks can be heated by dipping the part that goes around the thumb in very hot water to make it pliable. Push it up on the thumb until it is about halfway covering the thumbnail and halfway covering the skin above the nail.

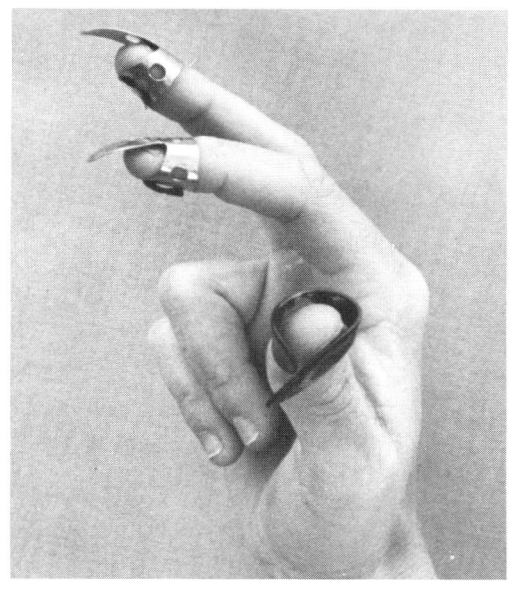
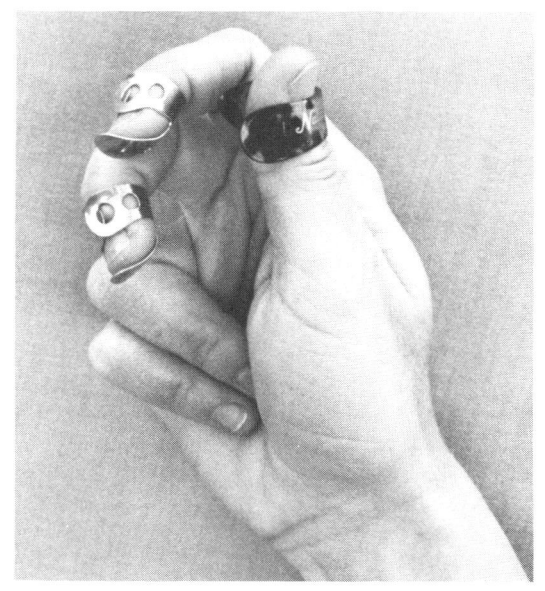

Incorrect   Correct

All of the picks should fit snugly. They should not slide on the finger when a string is plucked. There is little difference in the tone produced by metal and plastic thumbpicks. However, metal fingerpicks are recommended over plastic. Picks can be purchased at most music stores that deal in stringed instruments.

RIGHT-HAND POSITION

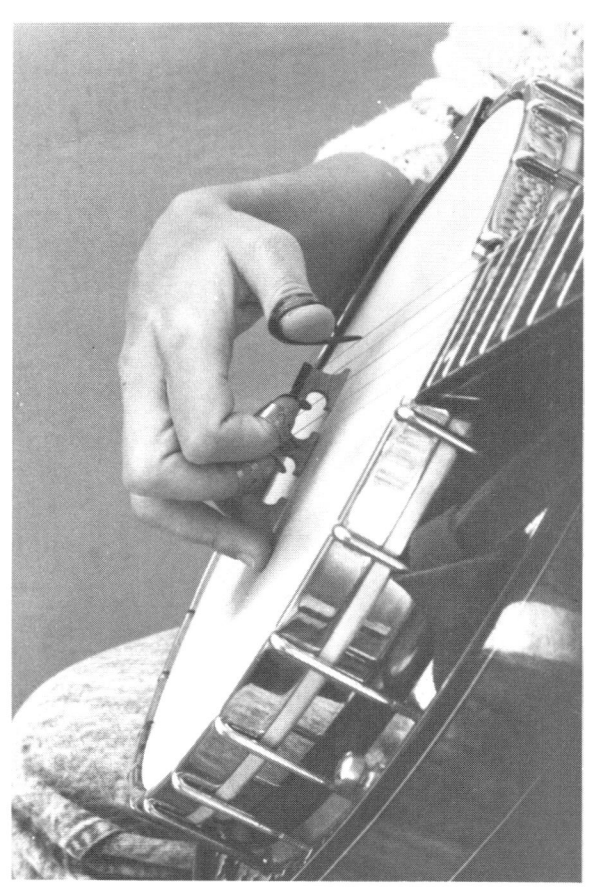 

The right hand should be held so that the middle finger strikes the string about an inch to an inch and a half from the bridge. Later you will learn to vary the tone by moving your hand closer to or farther from the bridge.

Both the ring and little finger should rest on the head of the banjo. Do not let the ring or little finger touch the bridge or the strings. It may take several days or even weeks to keep the ring finger down at all times, but keep trying. A small percentage of students will not be able to keep the ring finger down even after much effort. Don't worry if you find that you are one of these people as there are some great players who never anchor their ring finger. This in itself is not a crucial aspect of positioning. The important thing is that the right hand does not rock or jerk when playing.

The wrist should be slightly arched. Do not let the palm touch the head or the bridge. The inside of the forearm should rest securely on the arm rest. This contact point, coupled with the two fingers planted firmly on the head, will create a sturdy three-point support. The right hand and forearm should be well-stabilized but not tense. Let gravity do most of the work of anchoring the right hand.

The picks should strike the strings perpendicularly - that is, at a 90° angle to the string. This angle will produce the clearest tone with the least amount of pick noise. To do this, raise or lower the neck of the banjo so that the picking fingers strike the strings perpendicularly. Do not twist the wrist of the right hand unnaturally. The wrist will tire more quickly and may cramp or feel uncomfortable if it is twisted.

The picking fingers should be bent and <u>very</u> <u>close</u> to the strings. The less distance the finger has to move to strike the strings, the faster and more accurate your playing will be. Efficiency of motion is essential.

Be aware of the direction the pick is traveling when it strikes the string. Try picking from under the string and then move around until picking from on top. You will notice a clearer, louder, and richer tone at a particular angle. That will be the pick direction which should be practiced. Usually the best tone is produced by picking in a downward motion (from on top of the string) instead of sideways (across the string). This angle is best because it makes the string oscillate at an angle that is perpendicular to the surface of the head. This results in stronger vibrations being transmitted through the bridge to the head, which results in a louder and clearer tone.

READING TABLATURE

Banjo tablature consists of five lines. Each line represents one of the banjo strings. The first (top) line of tablature represents the first (bottom) string on the banjo. The second line represents the second (from the bottom) string, and so on.

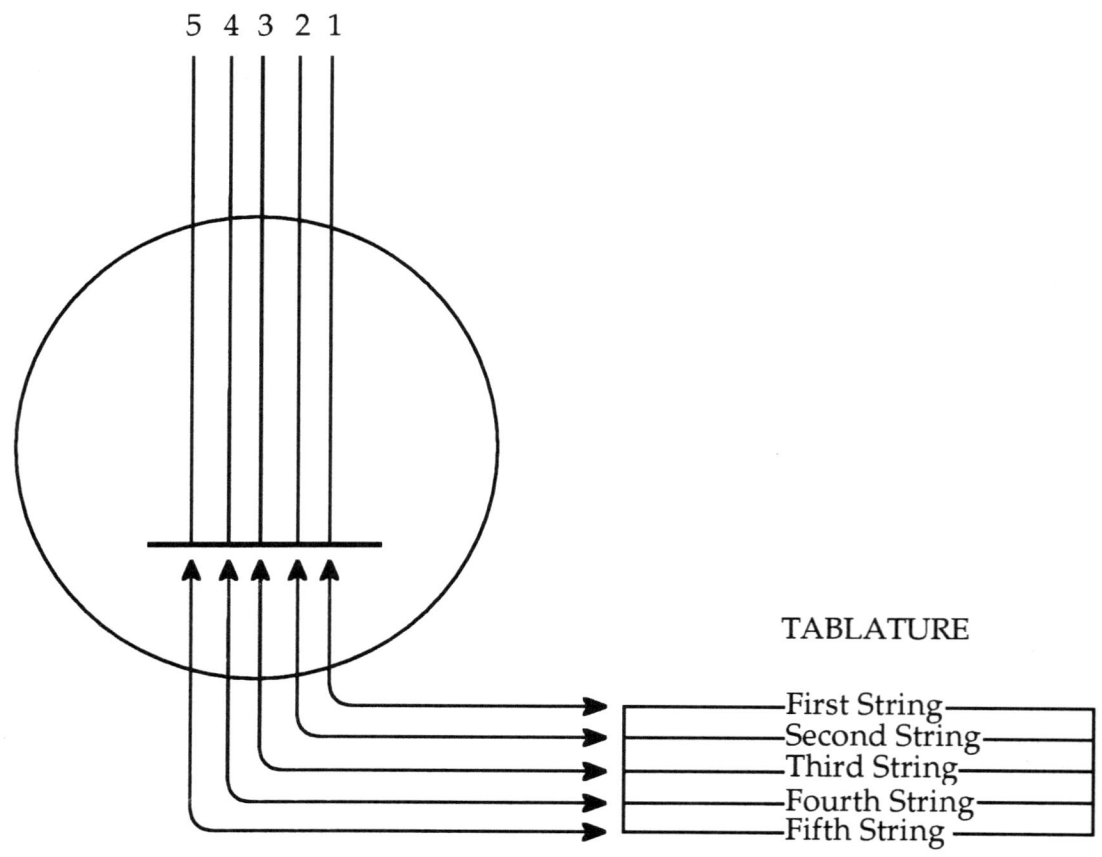

A number on one of the tablature lines shows which fret the left-hand finger is to be placed behind:

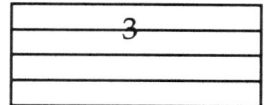

Play the second string while holding it behind the third fret.

A zero on one of the tablature lines means to play the designated string <u>open</u> (without fretting it):

Play the third string open.

A capital letter under the note designates which <u>right-hand</u> finger is to strike the string:

> T = Thumb
> I = Index
> M = Middle

In problem spots, a lower case letter may appear above the note showing which <u>left-hand</u> finger is to be used:

> i = index
> m = middle
> r = ring
> p = pinky

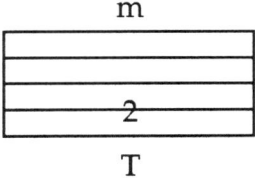

Play the fourth string, second fret. Use the Thumb of the right hand and the middle finger of the left hand.

Tricky or often-mistaken right-hand fingerings will be marked with a caution arrow (↑).

(This page is for notes, supplementary exercises or songs)

LESSON 1

THE ROLL

A Roll is a pattern used by the Right hand. Many rolls are employed by three-finger banjoists, but the easiest and probably the most useful is the Alternating Thumb Roll.

ALTERNATING THUMB ROLL

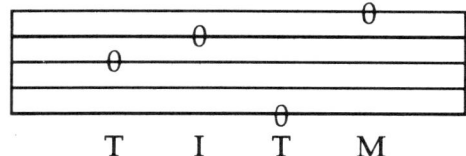

Practice this roll over and over, trying to space the notes evenly. Be sure not to play too fast. Start at a speed that is so slow that you can maintain exact equal spacing of the notes.

A roll has not been mastered until it can be performed automatically; it should be performed correctly without having to concentrate on the order of the fingers. A good test is to talk while playing the roll. If you can concentrate on talking and still play the roll correctly with equally-spaced notes, you are ready to use it in a song.

MELODY NOTES and FILL NOTES

Three-finger banjo music consists of an almost unbroken stream of fast notes. However, not all of these notes are of equal importance. Out of the seven or eight notes in each measure, only one or two (or sometimes three) actually carry the tune of the song. These are the notes you would pronounce a syllable on when singing the words to the song. These notes are called <u>Melody</u> <u>Notes</u>.

All of the other notes are called <u>Fill</u> <u>Notes</u>. The fill notes create a backdrop of sound, filling up the space between the melody notes and creating the machine-gun effect that is unique to bluegrass banjo style.

For the melody to be obvious to the listener, the banjoist must emphasize the melody notes. Emphasis is especially needed during the period when a song is in the middle stages of having been learned - when the information has been assimilated and the fingers are playing the right notes in the right sequence, but still at a slow rate of speed. Due to the nature of bluegrass banjo style, the melody automatically becomes more obvious as the speed increases. The problem facing the beginner is the fact that it may take weeks or even months before sufficient speed is attained to make the melody stand out. To remedy this problem, the melody notes will appear in <u>Bold</u> <u>Face</u> type in this book.

After a song is learned to the point of being fairly smooth and partially memorized, start playing the bold face notes louder than the surrounding fill notes. You will find that the tune will emerge from the seemingly unrelated succession of notes you have been playing.

In the later stages of learning a song, the melody notes are <u>all</u> that you should focus on. The song has been practiced so many times by this point that the fill notes will be played unconsciously. If you are <u>thinking</u> <u>the</u> <u>melody</u> instead of thinking mechanics, the listener will probably be able to hear the melody.

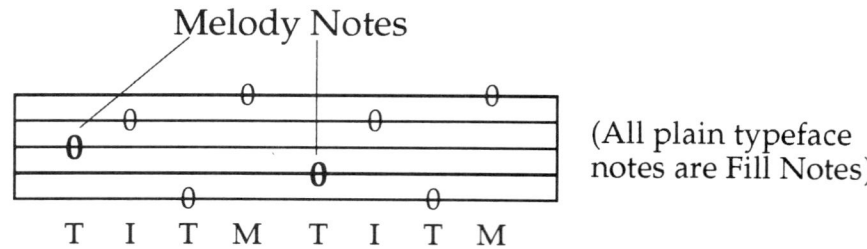

(All plain typeface notes are Fill Notes)

Practice the following exercise. Remember to <u>space the notes evenly</u>. Note that the first note of the third roll is played on the <u>fourth</u> string instead of the third string.

EXERCISE 1

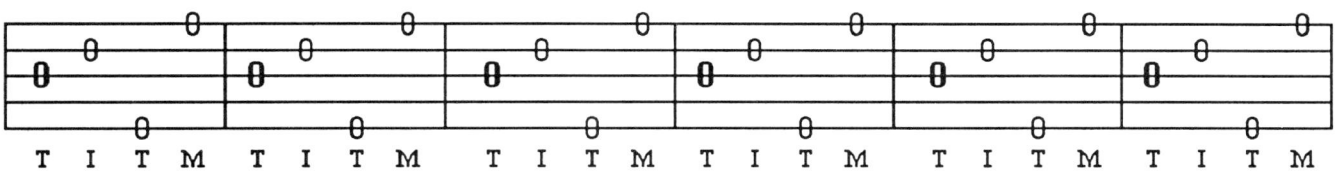

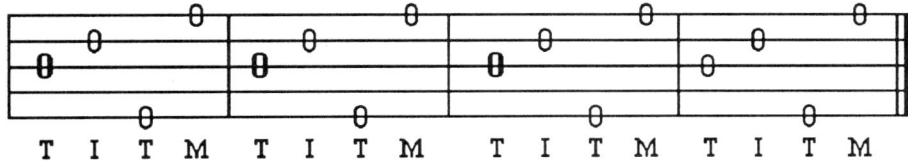

Repeat the exercise for several minutes at a time without leaving a space between rolls or at the end of the exercise.

LEFT-HAND POSITION

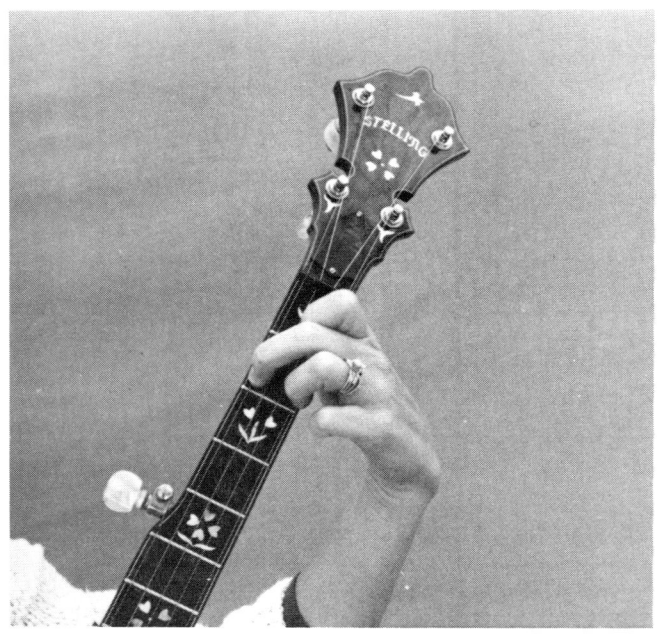

The left hand should be held so that the very tips of the fingers touch the strings. To do this, rest the thumb lightly on the back of the neck and keep the wrist straight or arched slightly away from the body. The neck should rest lightly in the V formed by the inside of the first knuckle of the index finger and the thumb.

<u>Do</u> <u>not</u> let the palm touch the neck. If the palm touches, it will make movement up and down the neck slow and awkward. In addition, the hand will tire more quickly because more muscles are being used. As long as the wrist is straight or arched slightly away from the body, the palm cannot touch and you will have optimum reach and agility.

Practice Exercise 1 until it can be performed smoothly. It would be best to memorize it. Then learn <u>Good Night Ladies</u> on the following page.

GOOD NIGHT LADIES
(Part One)

Traditional   Arranged by Jack Hatfield

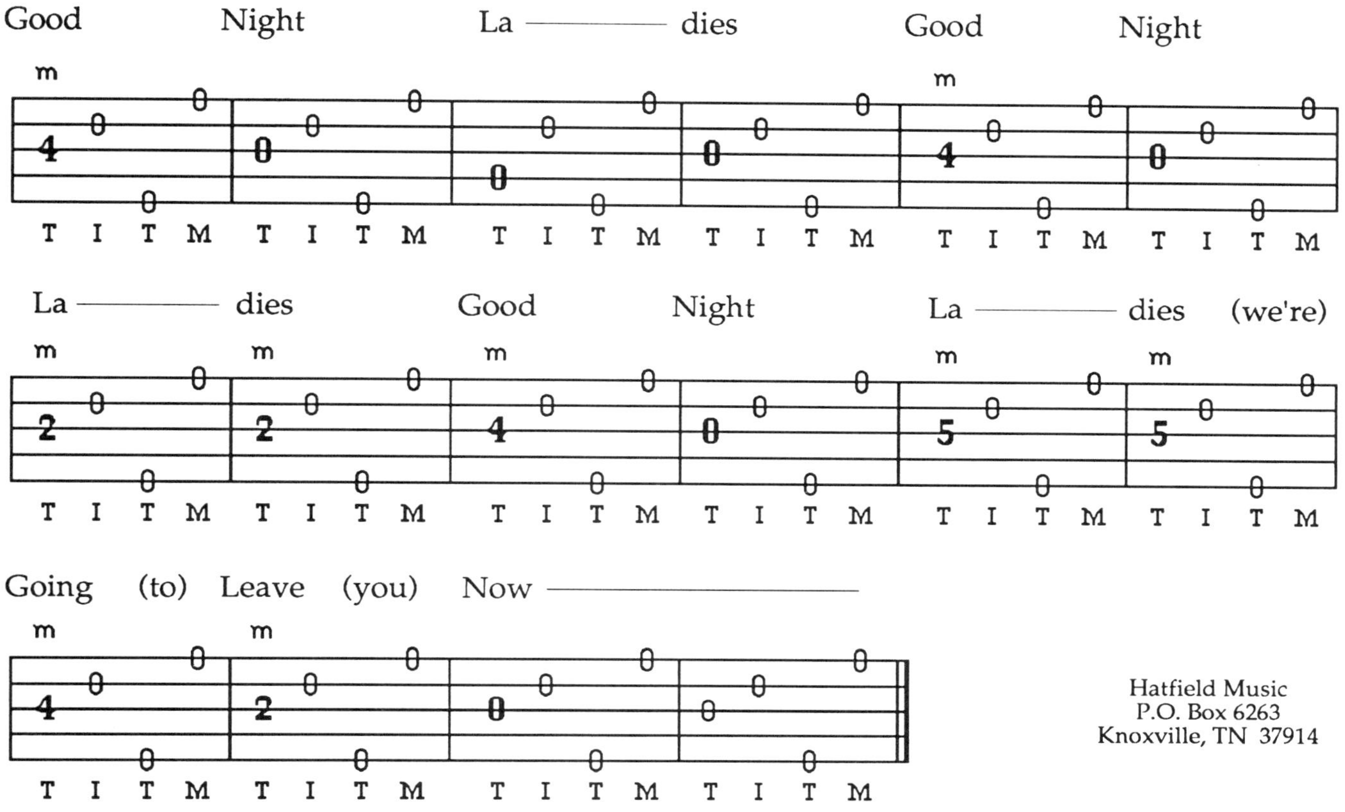

Hatfield Music
P.O. Box 6263
Knoxville, TN 37914

Repeat the song several times without pausing between rolls or at the end. Be sure to maintain an <u>equal</u> <u>amount</u> <u>of</u> <u>time</u> between <u>each</u> note.

If there are problem spots, extract those passages and play them repeatedly until each one can be performed smoothly. You can then resume practicing the song in its entirety.

LESSON 2

TWO SIMPLE CHORDS

G   **D⁷**

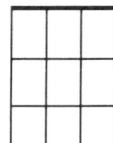  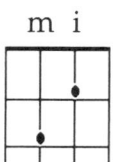 

*The banjo is tuned in open **G**, so no left-hand fingers are needed to form the **G** chord.*

The diagrams above are <u>Chord</u> <u>Diagrams</u>. The horizontal lines represent the frets. The bold line at the top represents the nut. The next horizontal line represents the first fret, the next line represents the second fret, and so on.

The vertical lines represent the strings. The first string is represented by the far right line, the second string is represented by the second line from the right, and so on. It is like holding your banjo in front of you in an upright position and looking at the area from the nut to the third fret.

The dots show where to place your left-hand fingers and the lower case letter above the diagram tells you which left-hand finger to use:

> i = index
> m = middle
> r = ring
> p = pinky

Note: The term "pinky" is used to avoid confusion. An "l" for "little" may be mistaken for an "i".

When fretting a string, use the very tip of the finger. For the best position, keep the fingernails closely trimmed. To get the clearest tone with the least effort, press down immediately <u>behind</u> the fret, but not on top of it.

If a muted or buzzing sound is heard when fretting a string, there could be several reasons:

    a) The string is being muted by a finger pressing the adjacent string. Keeping the wrist arched so the fingers come down perpendicular to the fretboard will remedy this.

    b) The fingertip is too far behind or on top of the fret.

    c) The finger is not supplying sufficient pressure.

    d) Long fingernails are inhibiting the fingertip from making firm contact.

    e) The banjo could have a worn fret or the neck could need adjusting.

From this point on, chord symbols will appear above the tablature. When a **G** chord is called for, you will either be fretting a single string or not using any left-hand fingers at all. When a **D⁷** chord is called for, you will usually be holding both fingers of the **D⁷** chord learned on the previous page.

Another **G** formation can be made by moving the **D⁷** chord fingering up two frets. This formation will be used in the following exercise.

The following exercise will help you learn to change chords smoothly while performing a roll. Remember to maintain an <u>equal amount of time</u> between each note. If you are unable to maintain equal spacing, you are probably playing too fast. Slow down to a speed at which you can play smoothly.

EXERCISE 2

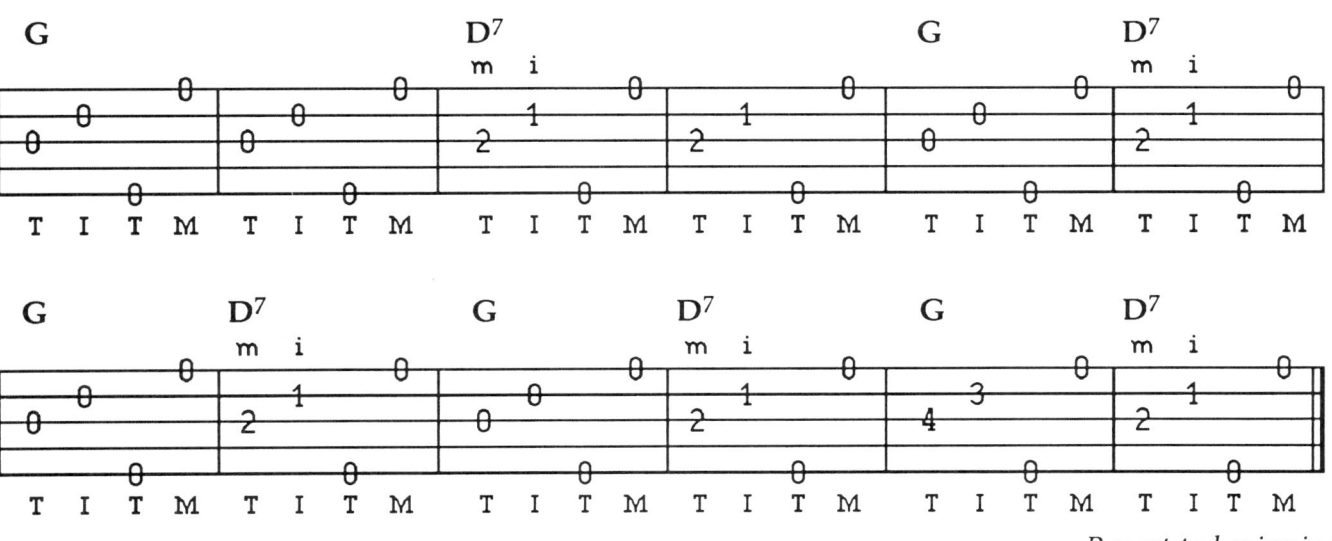

Repeat to beginning without pausing

In the following exercise, the thumb will not always play the fifth string on the third note of the roll as it did throughout GOOD NIGHT LADIES - Part One. Play through this exercise until you are comfortable using the thumb on the inside strings, then proceed to GOOD NIGHT LADIES - Part Two on the following page.

EXERCISE 3
Right-Hand Part to GOOD NIGHT LADIES - Part Two

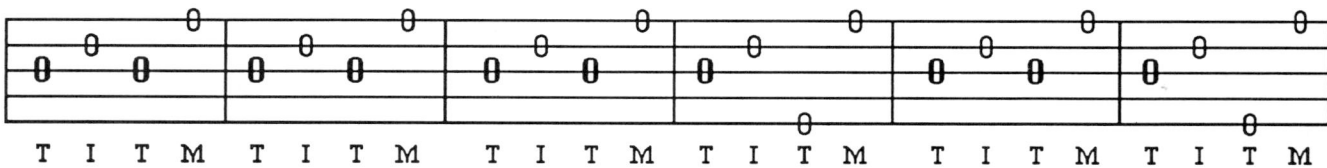

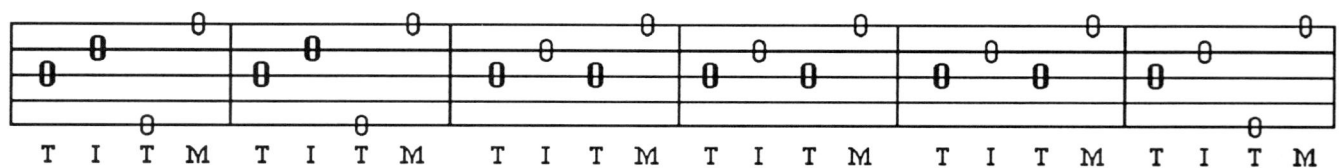

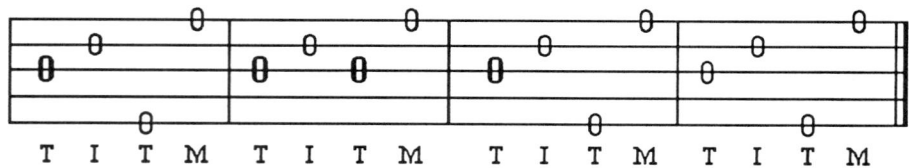

Remember, when moving from the **D⁷** to the **G** position in line two of the following arrangement, do not pick up the fingers - just relax the pressure somewhat and slide the **D⁷** chord up two frets without losing string contact.

Once this arrangement has been mastered, combine it with Part One that has already been learned. Proceed from Part One to Part Two with no hesitation, then start over again, playing the entire song several times through without stopping.

Remember - If you are making any mistakes, you are going too fast.

GOOD NIGHT LADIES
(Part Two)

Traditional

Arranged by Jack Hatfield

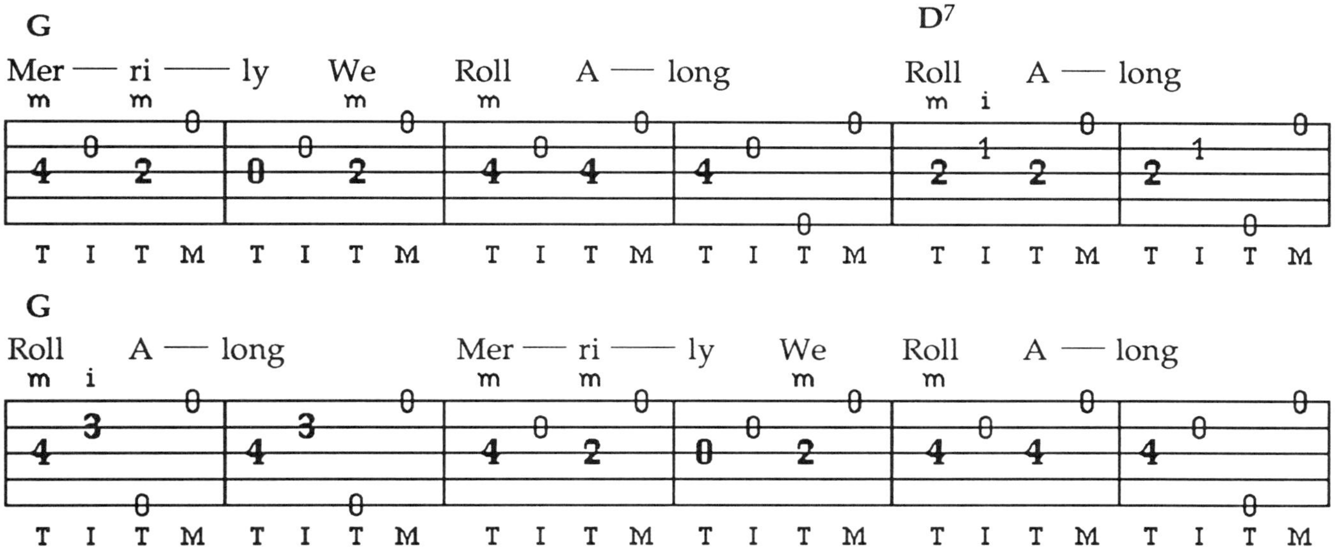

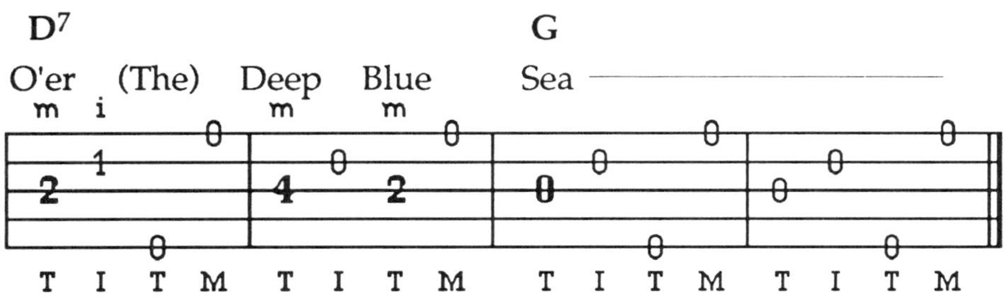

Hatfield Music
P.O. Box 6263
Knoxville, TN 37914

27

LESSON 3
THE FORWARD ROLL

The <u>Forward</u> <u>Roll</u> shown below is another extremely useful right-hand pattern. Most songs can be played with a combination of the Alternating Thumb and Forward rolls.

FORWARD ROLL

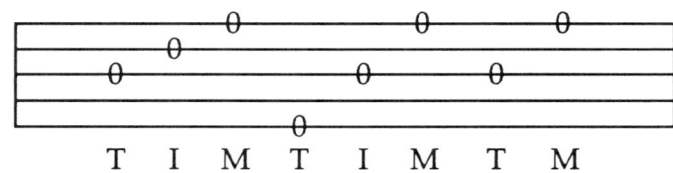

Practice this roll until you can perform it smoothly while talking, then proceed to the following song:

BOIL THEM CABBAGE

Traditional   Arranged by Jack Hatfield

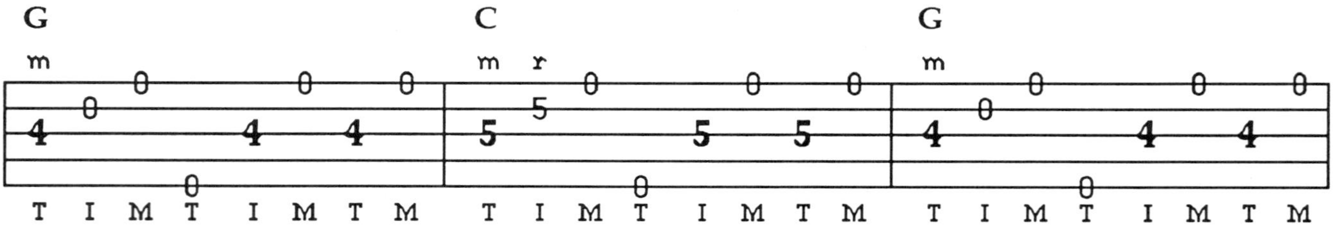

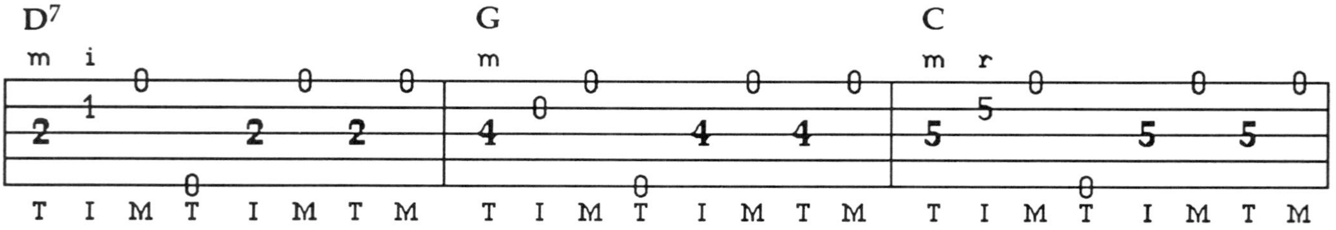

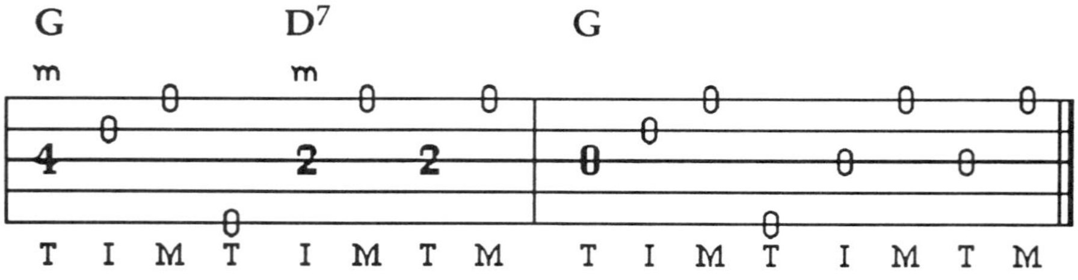

Note: It is more efficient to leave the middle finger of the left hand on the third string for the first seven rolls. Slide it from fret to fret rather than removing it and replacing it on the string.

28

LESSON 4

CHANGING STRINGS WITH THE FORWARD ROLL

Seldom will you be able to play an entire song using only the third string for the melody notes. It will take all three inside strings and sometimes the first string to render most melodies. The following exercise and song demonstrate this. Remember - Although the melody notes change strings, the roll pattern does not vary. A roll is defined by <u>the sequence of the Right -Hand fingers</u>, not by the choice of strings played.

EXERCISE 4
Right-Hand Part to <u>TOM DOOLEY</u>

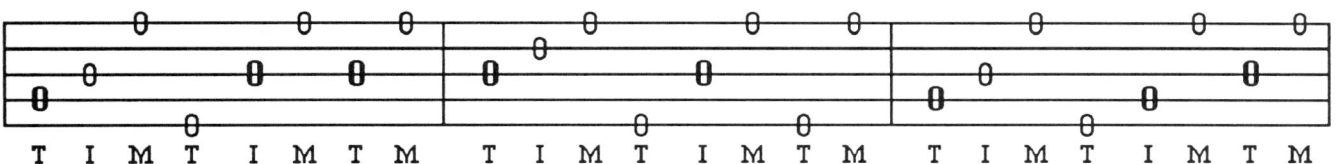

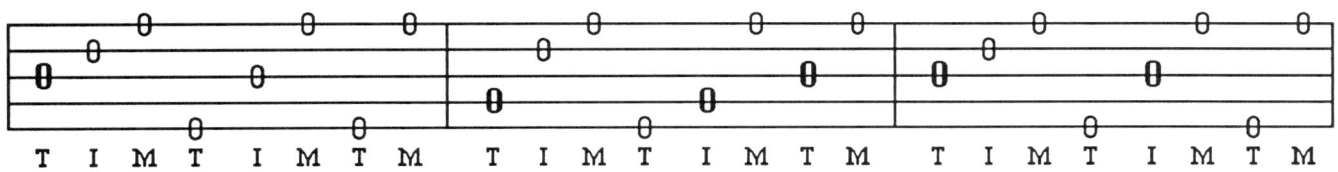

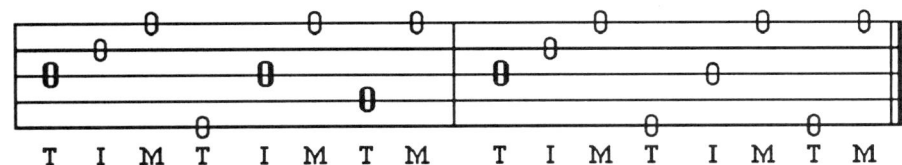

Repeat over and over, spacing all notes evenly. Do not pause before repeating.

TOM DOOLEY

Traditional Arranged by Jack Hatfield

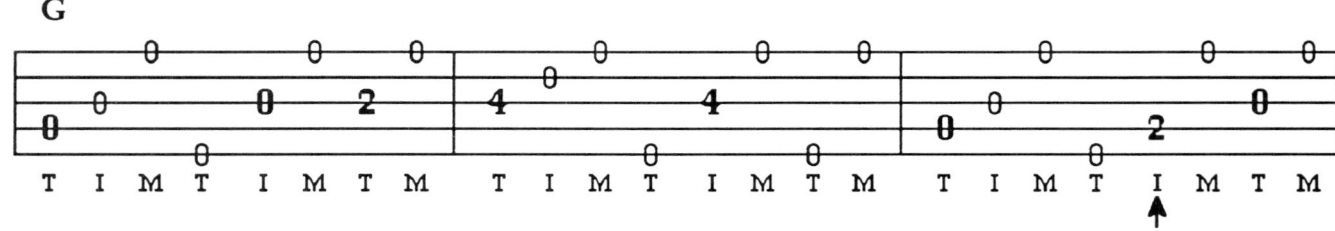

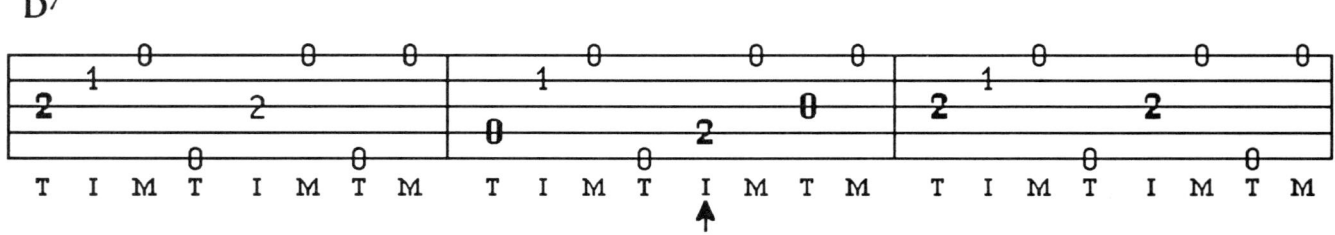

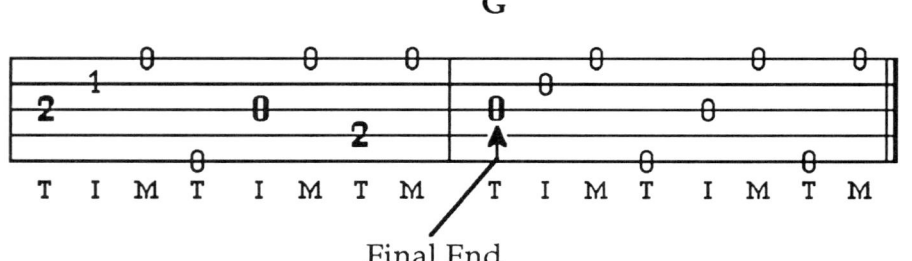

To end the song, stop on the note marked "Final End"

Final End

NOTES:

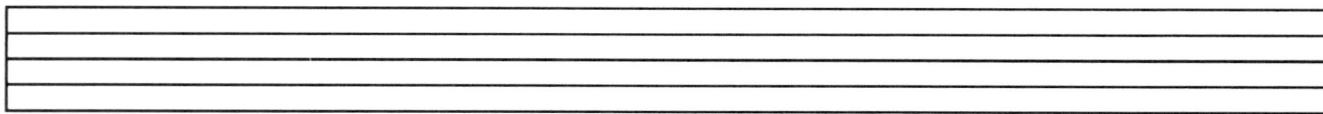

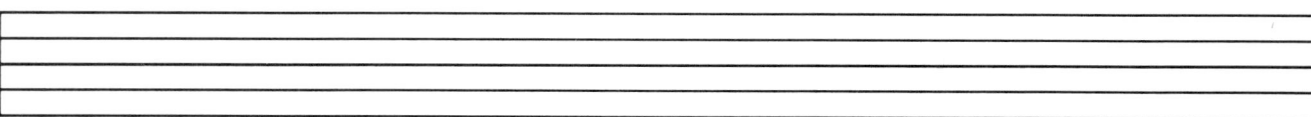

LESSON 5

COUNTING TIME

Until now, all songs and exercises have been practiced with equal spacing between the notes. However, there are times when there must be more space left after some notes. Reasons for doing this can be:

   a) To accent a melody note.
   b) To give the left hand time to change positions.
   c) To mark the end of a musical phrase.

A few musical terms must be defined before we learn to count time and start varying the duration of notes.

A <u>beat</u> is a unit of time. Within a song, all beats are equal in duration.

A <u>measure</u> or <u>bar</u> is a larger unit of time consisting of a given number of beats. Most banjo tablature is divided into four-beat measures. Dividing the music into measures makes it easier to count time and keep your place.

The dotted lines in the sample measure pictured below will help you visualize how each measure is divided into four equal parts. Each part represents one beat.

ONE MEASURE

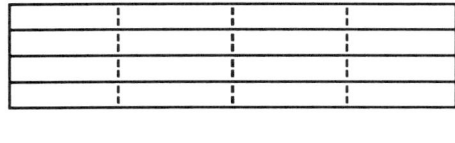

Beats: 1   2   3   4

A <u>quarter</u> <u>note</u> is a note that lasts one beat. Its name is based on the fact that it lasts <u>one</u> <u>quarter</u> of a measure. The quarter note will be shown in banjo tablature as a note with a vertical stem. Quarter notes will stand alone, unconnected to any other notes.

It takes four quarter notes to fill up a measure. To count quarter notes, say *one, two, three,* or *four* depending on which beat of the measure is being occupied.

QUARTER NOTES

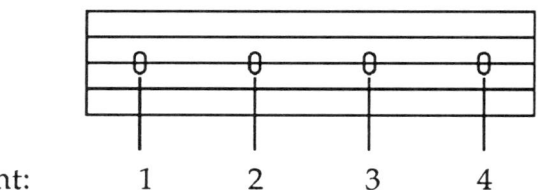

Count: 1   2   3   4

An <u>eighth</u> <u>note</u> is a note that lasts one half of a beat. In addition to having a vertical stem, the eighth note will also have a horizontal beam connecting it with other eighth notes. Eighth notes almost always occur in groups of two or four. On the rare occasion that an eighth note appears by itself, it will have a flag on the end of its vertical stem.

LONE EIGHTH NOTE

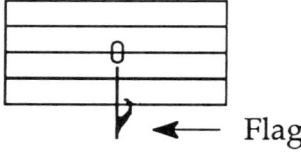 ← Flag

To count eighth notes, count the note occupying the first half of the beat as *one, two, three,* or *four* depending on where it is in the measure. Count any note occurring on the second half of any beat as *and* (&).

EIGHTH NOTES

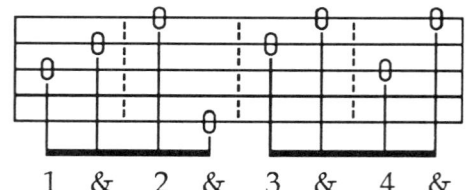

Count: 1 & 2 & 3 & 4 &

Quarter notes and eighth notes can be mixed within the measure, but each measure will <u>always</u> <u>contain</u> <u>four</u> <u>full</u> <u>beats</u>. The only exception is when there are *pick-up* notes at the beginning of a song.

QUARTER NOTES and EIGHTH NOTES MIXED

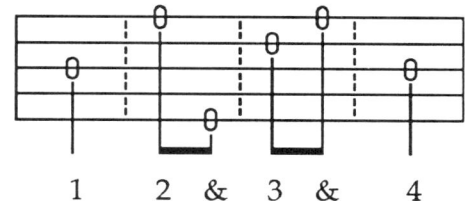

1   2 & 3 &   4

Since an eighth note occupies one half a beat and a quarter note occupies a full beat, you could think of eighth notes as being <u>twice</u> <u>as</u> <u>fast</u> as quarter notes.

Up to this point in the book all notes played have been eighth notes, although they were not shown with stems and beams. The proper timing symbols will be used in the arrangements which follow.

EXERCISE 5

Directions: In the sample tablature below, fill in the count under each note with a pencil and let your instructor or another knowledgable person check your understanding of counting time (this is an extremely important aspect of music and the student should not continue until it is clearly understood). Play the exercise below, making sure that all beats are equal and that the quarter notes last exactly twice as long as the eighth notes.

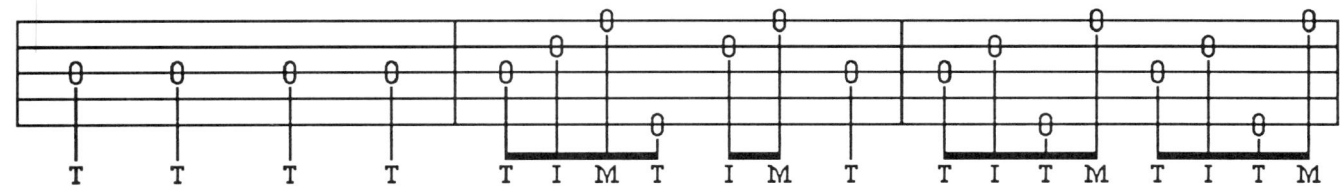

Count:

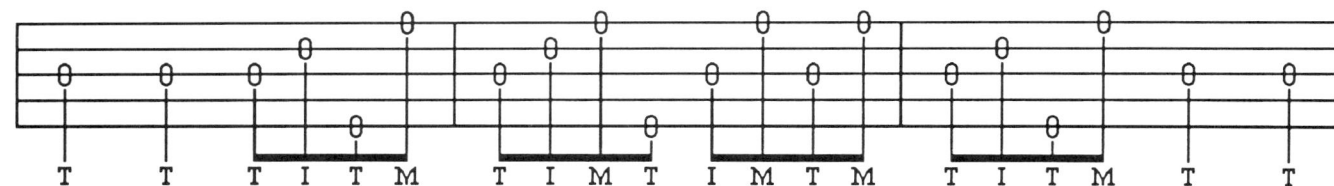

Count:

LESSON 6

THE PINCH

The Pinch is a space-filler and musical punctuation mark, like the period at the end of a sentence. At the end of a musical phrase, there is usually a pause of one to three beats before the next phrase begins. Using a Pinch to fill this void makes it more obvious that the phrase has ended while also maintaining the constant flow of notes required in three-finger style playing. The Pinch is done by simultaneously picking the first and fifth strings with the Middle and Thumb, respectively.

THE PINCH

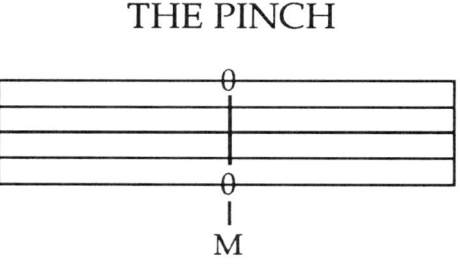

Proceed to the exercise on the following page. To practice the newly-learned skill of counting time, it would be a good idea to write in the count under each note and let your instructor or other expert check your work. Then learn to play the exercise, making sure that all of the beats are equally spaced and that the quarter notes last exactly twice as long as the eighth notes. When you are ready, learn Sourwood Mountain.

NOTES:

EXERCISE 6
Right-Hand Part to SOURWOOD MOUNTAIN

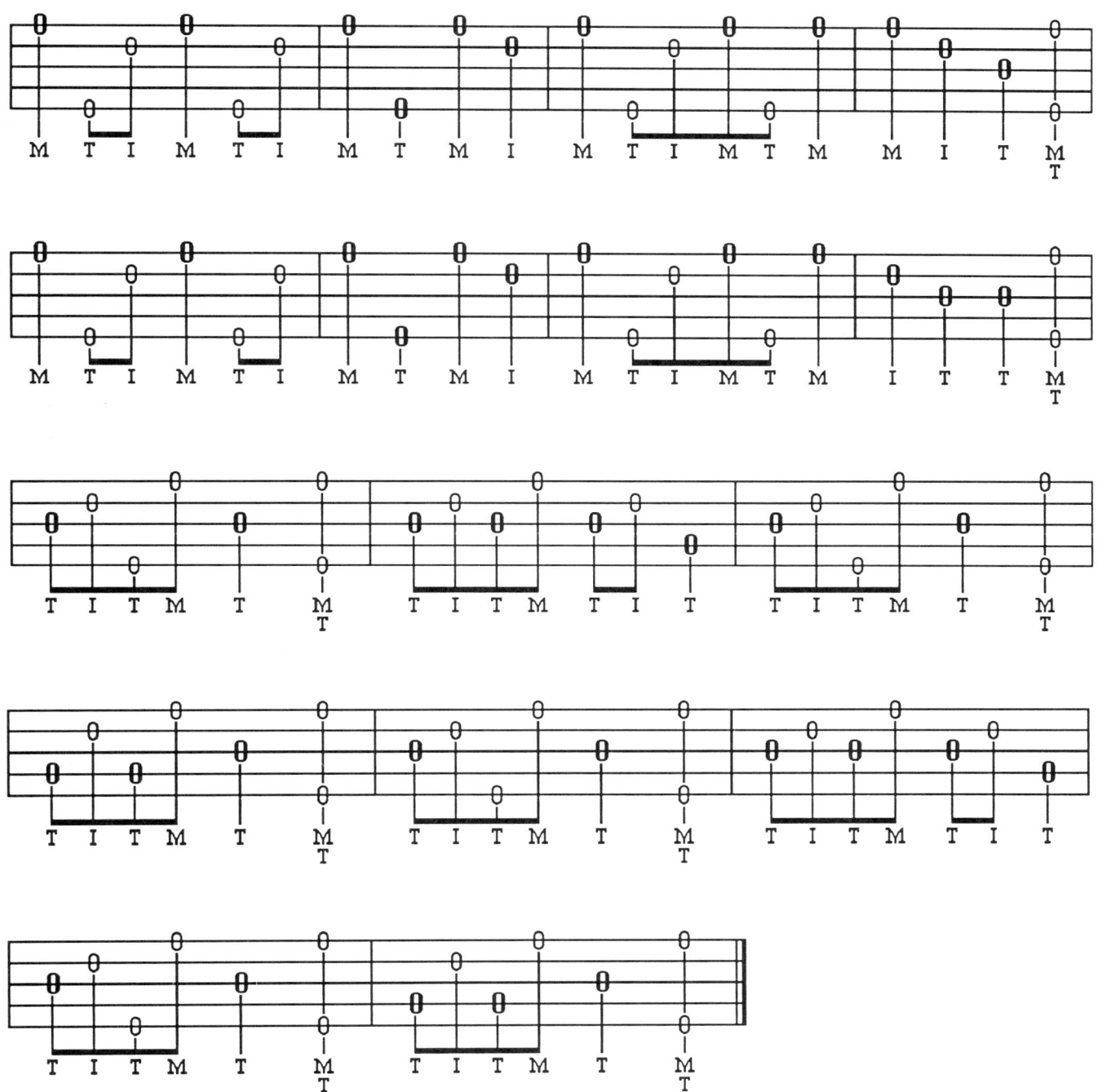

SOURWOOD MOUNTAIN

Traditional   Arranged by Jack Hatfield

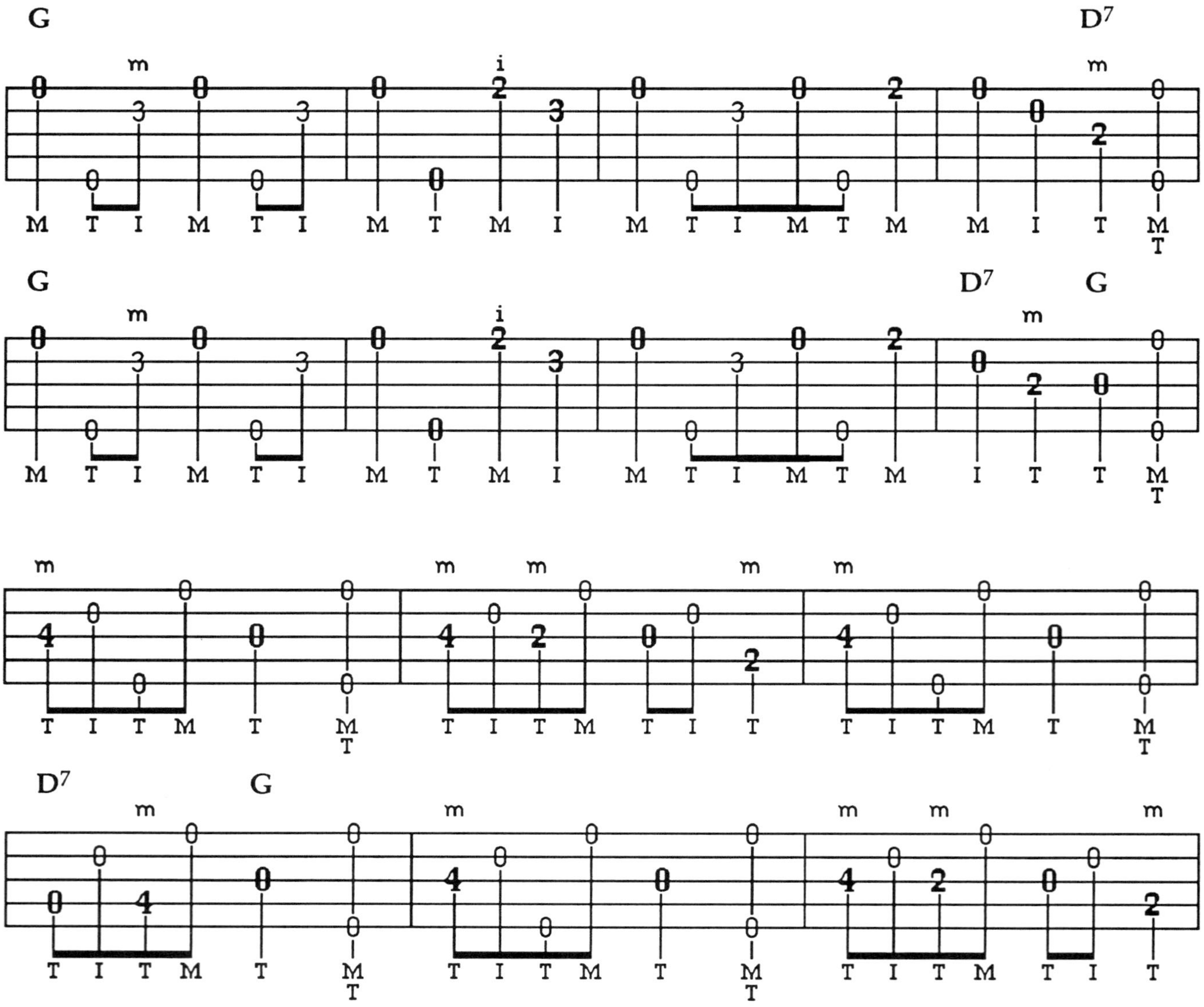

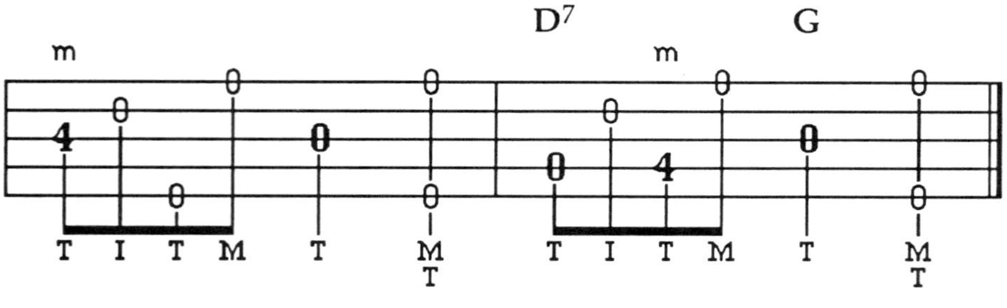

Hatfield Music
P.O. Box 6263
Knoxville, TN 37914

LESSON 7

PICK-UP NOTES

Sometimes there will be a partial measure at the beginning of a tune. These notes are called <u>Pick-up Notes</u>. The purpose of <u>Pick-up Notes</u> is:

a) To signal the accompanying musicians as to when they should start playing.

b) To set the tempo (the speed at which the Pick-up Notes are played is the speed which will be maintained throughout the tune).

c) To fill in space between the end of the song and the beginning when repeating the tune. In the example below, the last partial measure plus the Pick-up Notes equals four beats (a full measure).

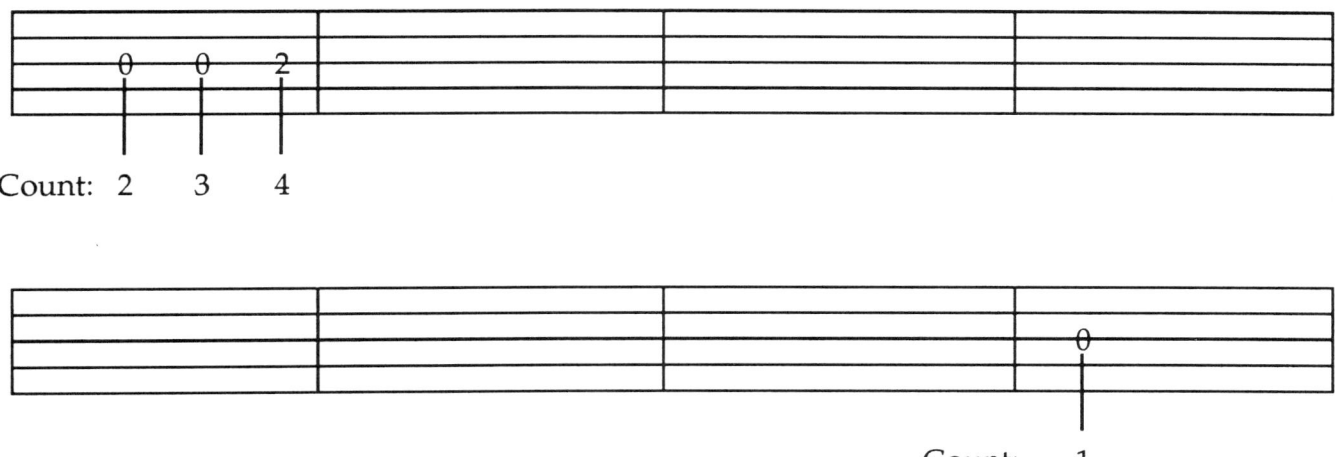

Proceed to the right-hand part of <u>Two Dollar Bill</u>. Be sure to count, playing the first pick-up note on the count of *two*.

EXERCISE 7
Right-Hand Part to TWO DOLLAR BILL

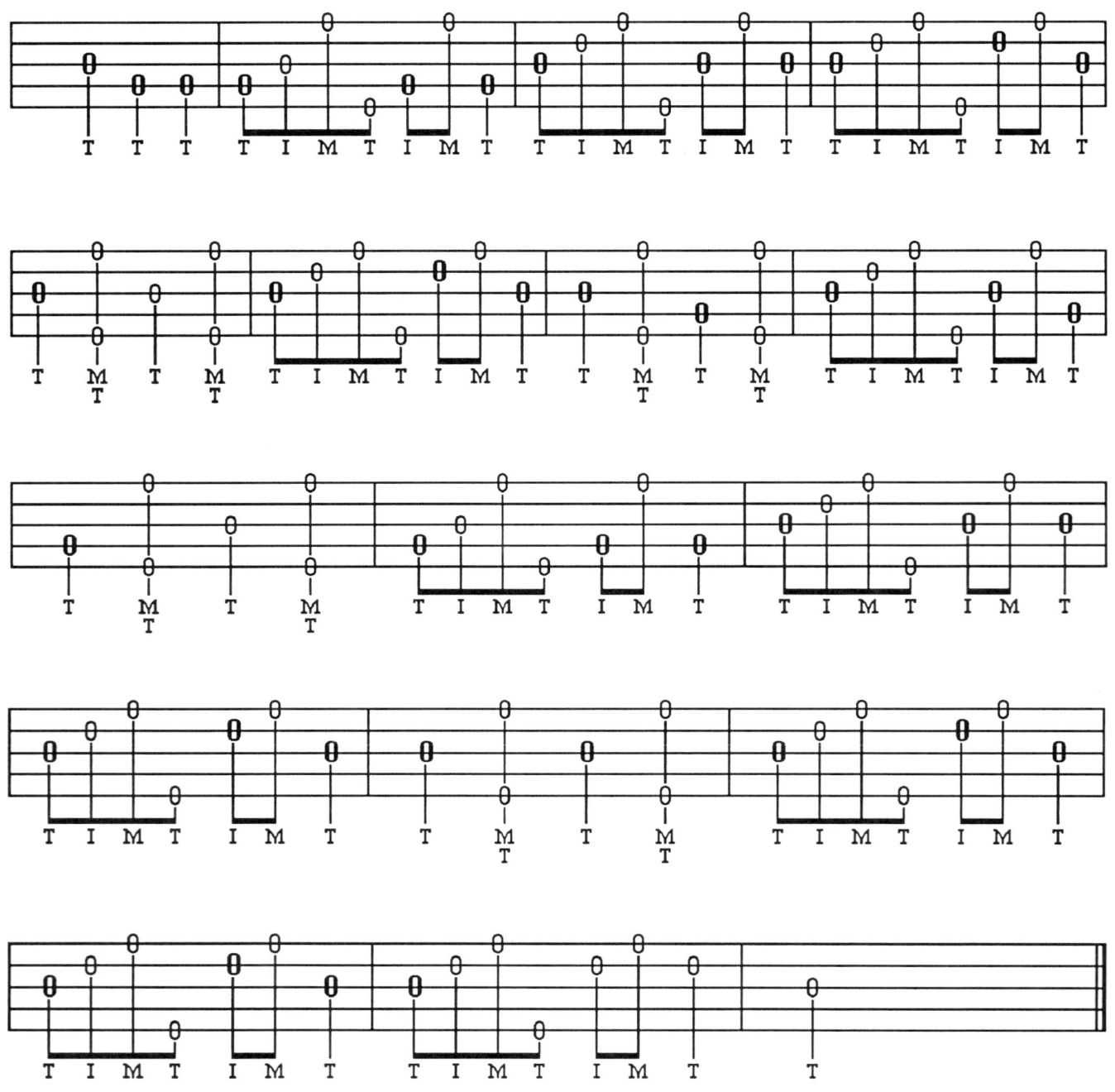

The **C** chord must be learned to play the following song. To do this, practice changing from **G** to **C** to **D⁷** while maintaining a roll.

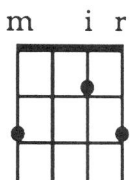
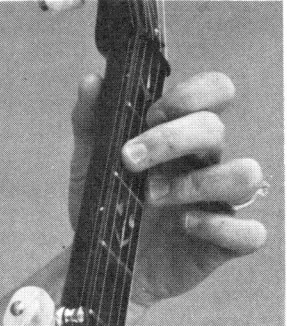

C Chord

TWO DOLLAR BILL

Traditional

Arranged by Jack Hatfield

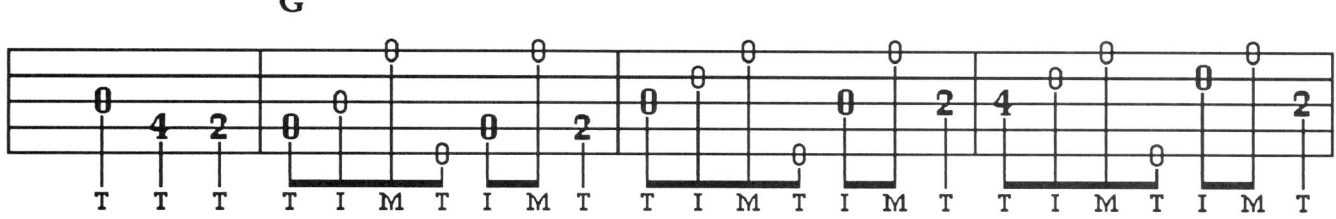
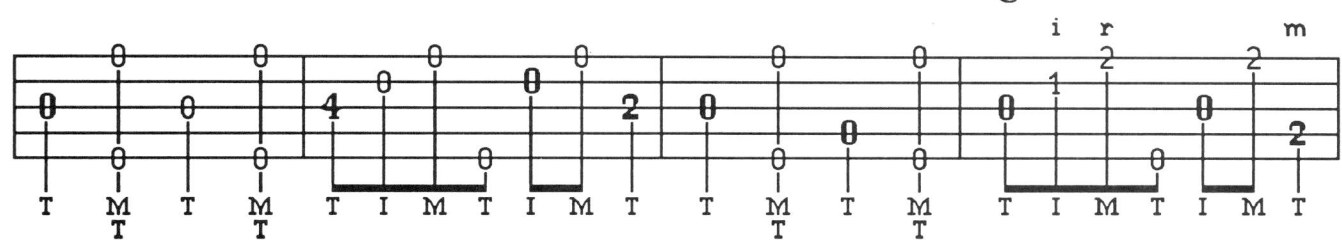
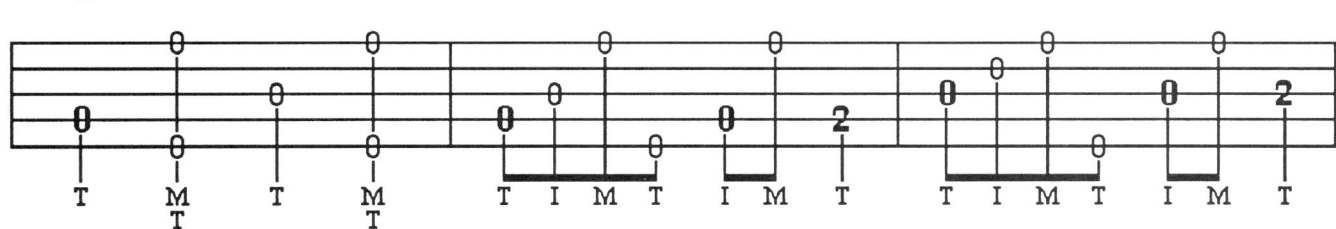
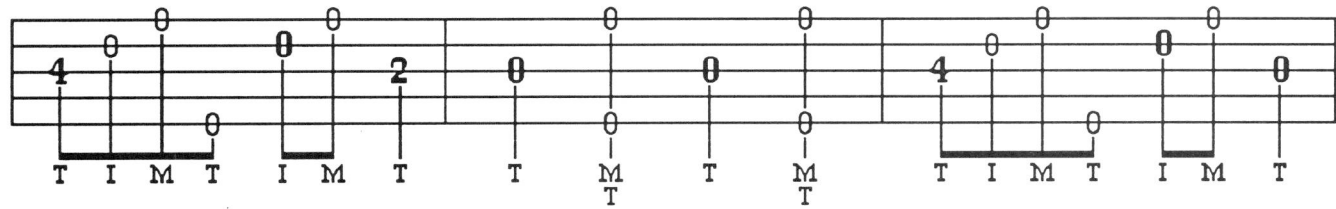
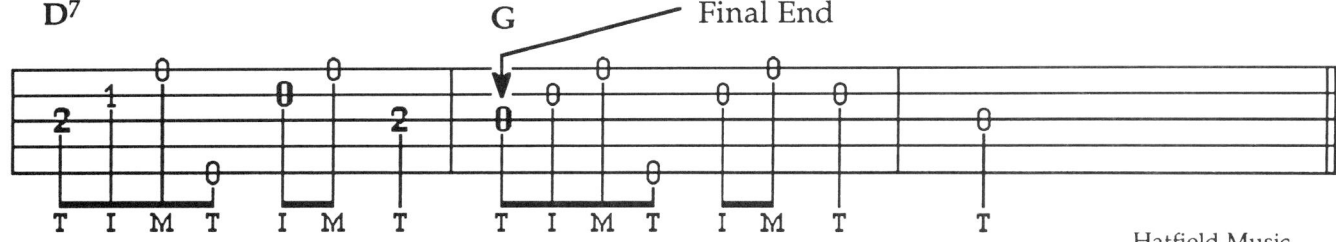

Hatfield Music
P.O. Box 6263
Knoxville, TN 37914

LESSON 8

FORWARD ROLL #2

To qualify as a Forward Roll, a one measure pattern must have two T I M sequences. The following is another example of a Forward Roll:

FORWARD ROLL #2

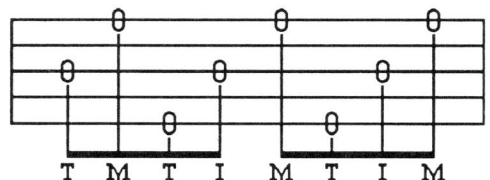

Practice this pattern until you can perform it smoothly and accurately while talking, then proceed to Exercise 8 and <u>My Old Kentucky Home</u> - Part One. First, however, learn the following very important principle:

ASSIGNING LEFT-HAND FINGERS

Up to this point fingering of the left-hand has been accomplished primarily with the index and middle fingers, because they are the strongest and most coordinated. In the interest of speed and efficiency, it is time to introduce some new ideas regarding the left hand.

A general rule for fingering is: the index finger will be used for any note on the first fret; the middle finger will be used for any note on the second fret; the ring finger will be used for any note on the third fret; and the pinky will be used for any note on the fourth fret. Use this finger assignment guideline no matter which string is being played. There will be many exceptions to this guideline, as in cases where two strings must be noted at the same fret at the same time (the **C** chord is an example). Adhere to these finger assignments throughout the remainder of this book unless an exception is noted in lower case letters above the tablature.

EXERCISE 8
Right-Hand Part to MY OLD KENTUCKY HOME Using Forward Roll #2

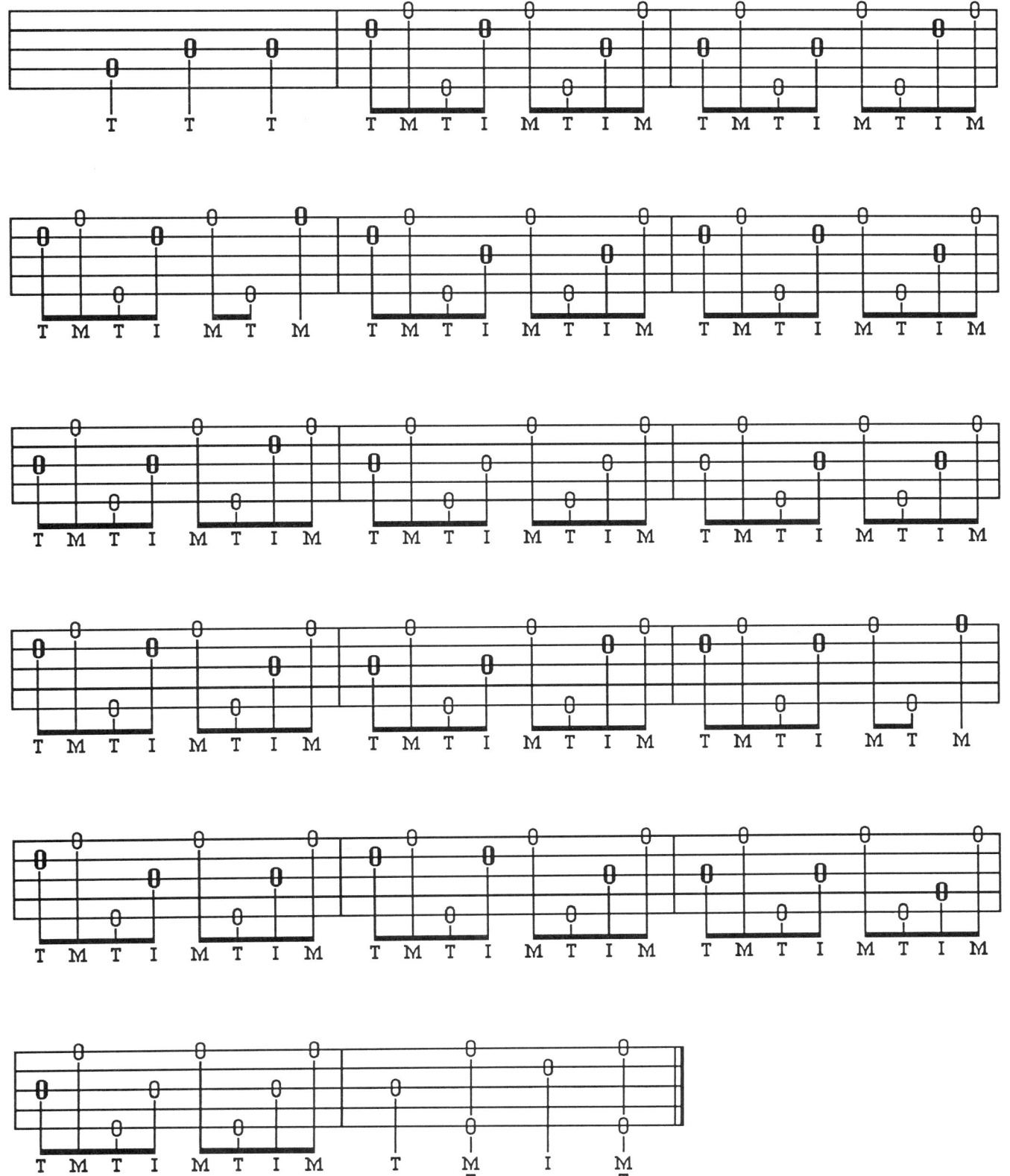

MY OLD KENTUCKY HOME

Stephen Foster

(Verse)

Arranged by Jack Hatfield

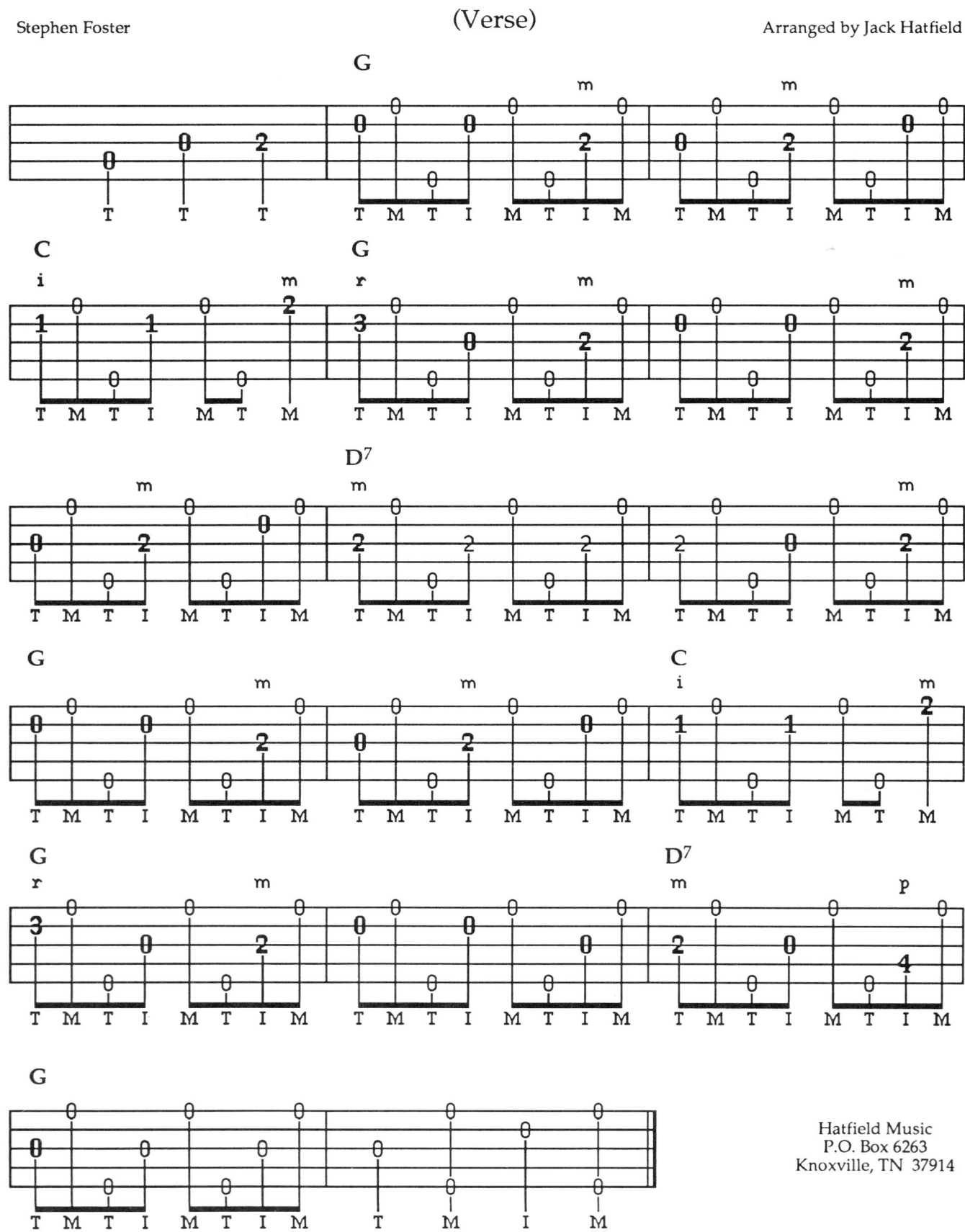

Hatfield Music
P.O. Box 6263
Knoxville, TN 37914

LESSON 9
A SIMPLE ENDING LICK
(The *Tag Lick*)

It is common practice to use an <u>Ending</u> or <u>Tag</u> Lick when a tune is finished. Like the pinch, the Tag Lick is a signal or musical punctuation mark. Below is an easy Tag Lick which can be used with any song. The first note of the Tag Lick is the last melody note of the song. In other words, it is the last note a syllable would be enunciated on when singing the melody.

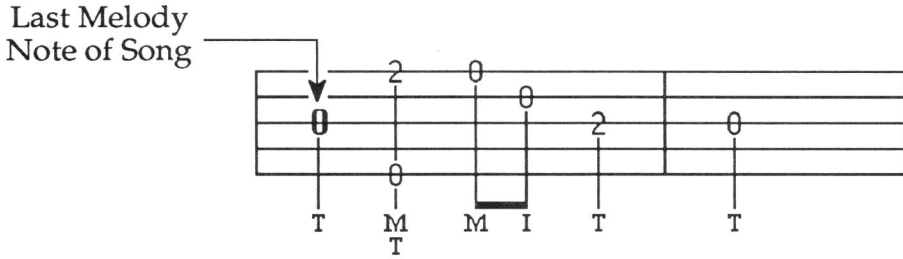

Repeat the Tag Lick and "filler" roll below over and over without stopping or pausing:

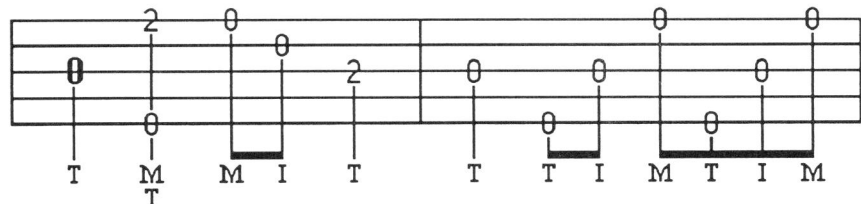

OMITTING FILL NOTES

Generally speaking, the fill note that appears on the last half of the first beat or the last half of the fourth beat can be omitted. This draws attention to the melody note that usually occurs on the downbeat of *one* or the downbeat of *four*, making the melody more obvious. It also gives you time to catch up if you happen to be behind the beat. Lastly, it breaks the monotony of the steady stream of eighth notes.

Now learn Exercise 9 and the chorus to <u>My</u> <u>Old</u> <u>Kentucky</u> <u>Home</u>. When you can play the chorus as fast and smoothly as the verse, combine the two.

EXERCISE 9
Right-Hand Part of Chorus to <u>MY</u> <u>OLD</u> <u>KENTUCKY</u> <u>HOME</u>
Note: The second note of Forward Roll #2 has been omitted

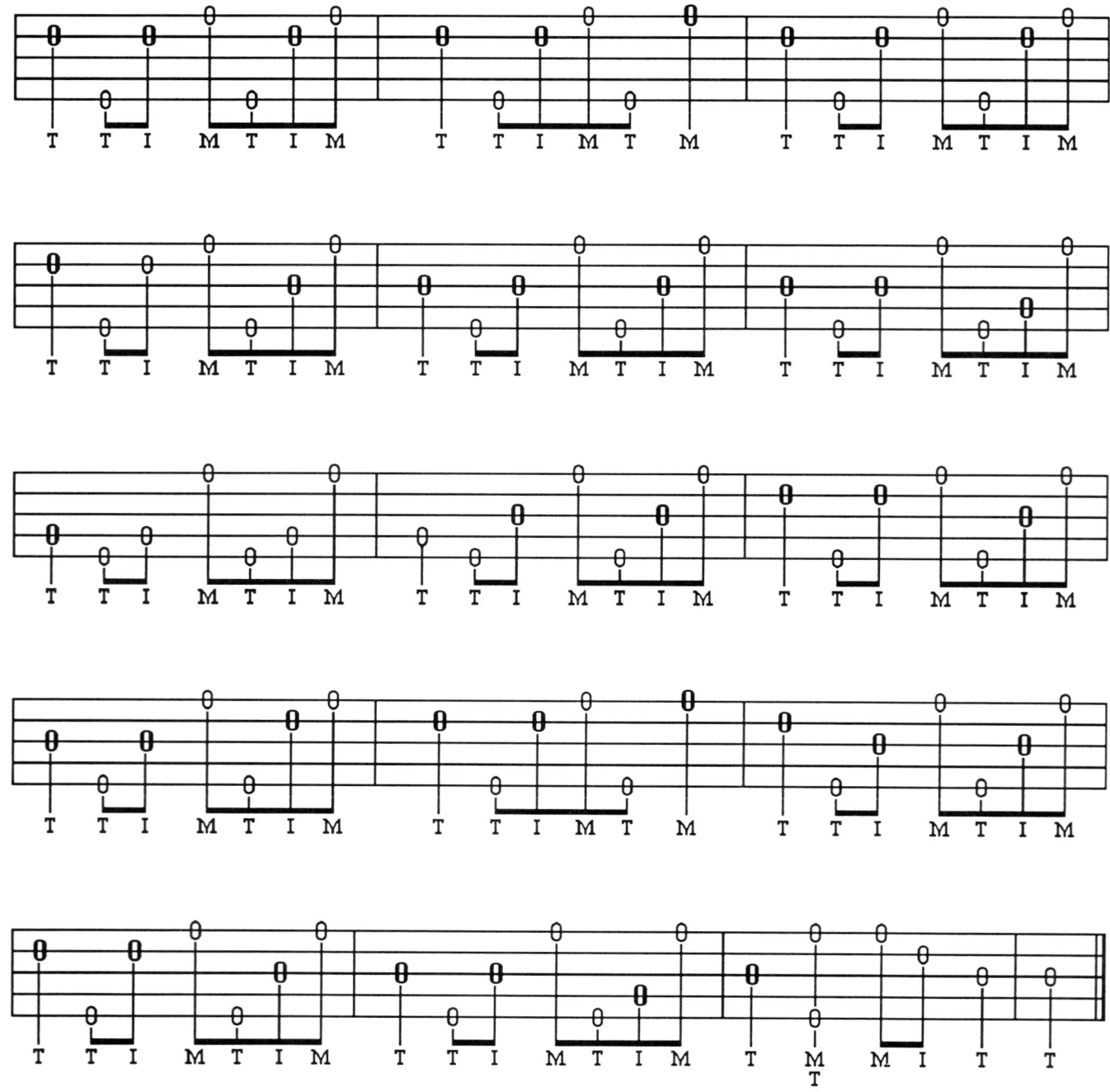

44

MY OLD KENTUCKY HOME
(Chorus)

Stephen Foster
Arranged by Jack Hatfield

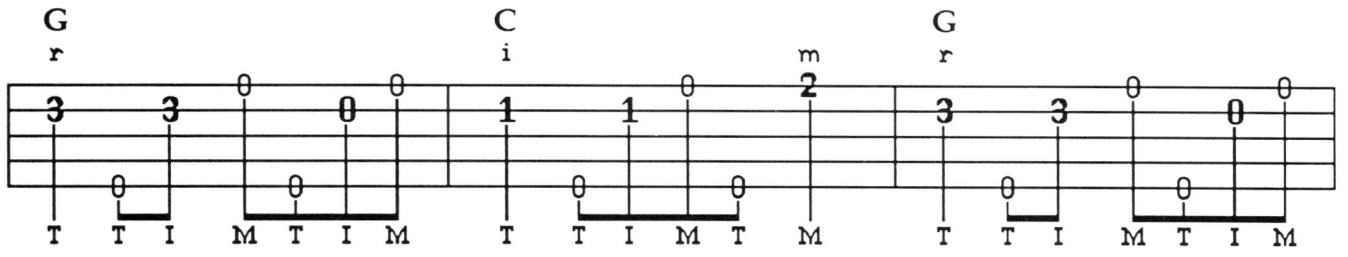
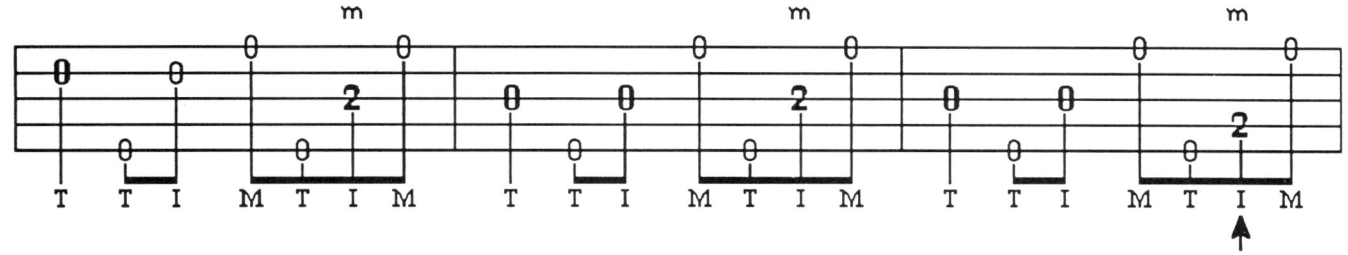
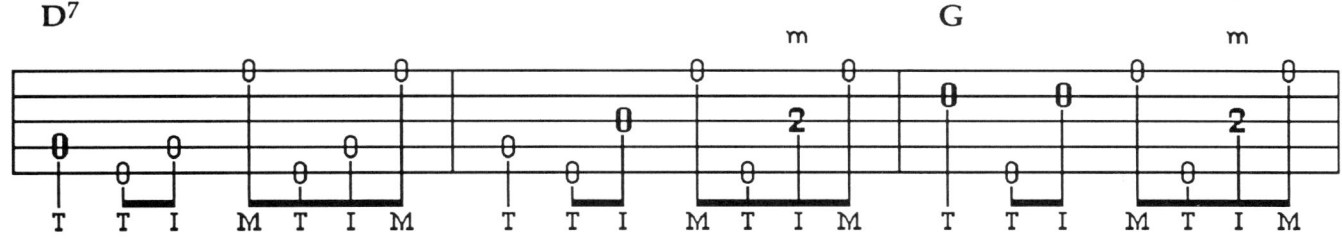
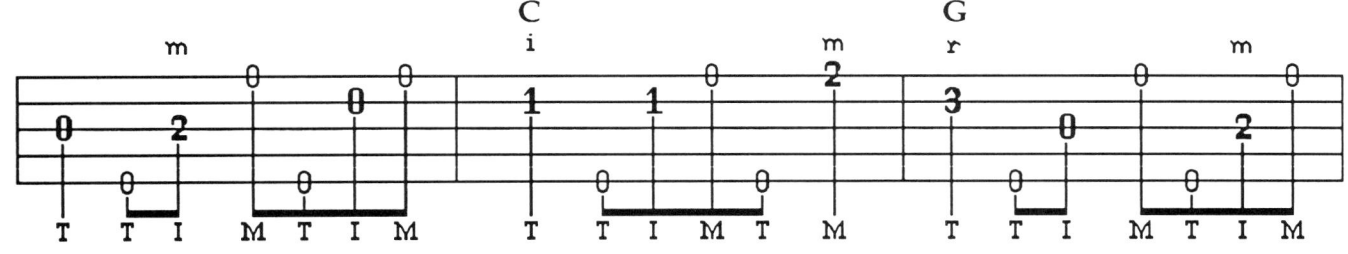
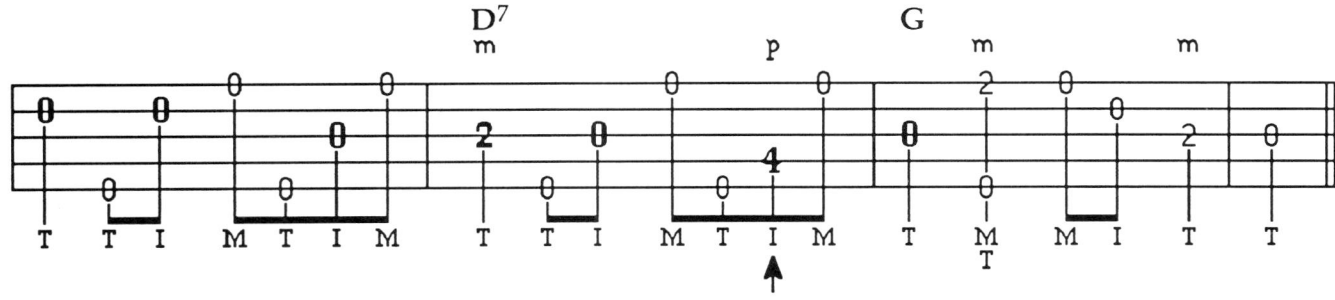

(Ending Lick)

Hatfield Music
P.O. Box 6263
Knoxville, TN 37914

PRACTICING EFFECTIVELY

The more something is practiced, the better it is performed. This fact is true for baseball, ballet, and banjo picking. Your rate of progress is directly related to how much time you spend "woodshedding" it.

Practicing an hour a day is advised. The hour could be divided into two half hour sessions at first to avoid fatigue. Make the practice session a part of your daily schedule, just like taking a bath or eating dinner. This routine requires discipline at first, but as time goes on it will become habit. It just takes a few weeks of conditioning. Do not feel the banjo <u>has</u> to be laid down after sixty minutes, though. If you are feeling good and having fun, continue until tired.

It is best to play easy well-known material for the first few minutes of the practice session as "warm up". Just like an athlete, the musician must loosen up his muscles and joints. Play slowly and smoothly on these tunes for ten to fifteen minutes. When you feel ready, spend twenty or thirty minutes playing the latest lesson and songs which are "in the works", concentrating on the weak points. Extract the difficult parts and work on them separately until they can be played correctly at a moderate speed. Try to memorize each piece to avoid being slowed down by looking back and forth from the tablature to your hands. Do not play a song through once and then go on to something else. Repeat each song several times without stopping. The repetition will increase your speed and smoothness.

For the last twenty minutes or so of your practice session, play the songs you enjoy the most of the ones you have mastered. Do not be too hard on yourself during this segment of your practice, just have fun. Hopefully, playing your favorite songs last will cause you to run over your allotted sixty minutes, resulting in bonus practice time and added improvement.

Your repertoire should be limited to a few tunes at first. After learning the rolls and chords a particular song is composed of, you may choose to discard that tune for a while to make time for the newer lessons. That tune can always be relearned at a later time if desired. However, always reserve a few tunes as favorites which you do play every day. These are the songs which will provide you with breakthroughs in technique and speed.

NOTES:

LESSON 10
REPEAT MARKS

A <u>Repeat</u> <u>Mark</u> is composed of a heavy vertical line and a thin vertical line accompanied by two dots. If there are two repeat marks with the dots facing each other, repeat everything between the marks. If there is only one repeat mark with the two dots to the left of the thin line, repeat back to the beginning of the song or section of the song.

Two repeat marks: repeat everything between the dots.

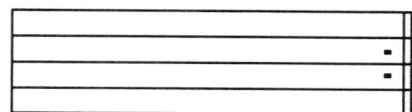

Single repeat mark: repeat back to the beginning of the song or section.

DOUBLE ENDINGS

A <u>Double</u> <u>Ending</u> will sometimes be used in conjunction with repeat marks. The first time a passage is played, the notes in the measure or measures under the *First Ending* will be played followed by a return to the beginning of the song or section. The second time the passage is played, skip over the notes under the first ending and play the notes under the *Second Ending* instead.

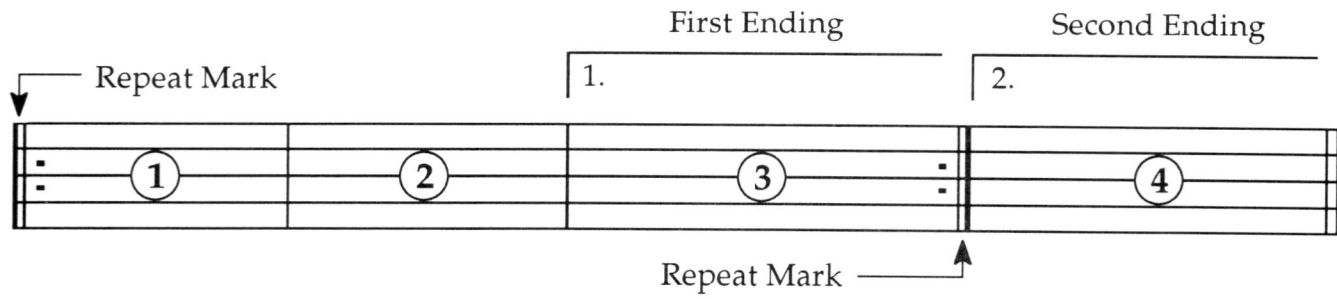

The playing order in the example above would be: measures 1; 2; 3; then measures 1; 2; 4.

In the next arrangement, Forward Roll #2 has been altered by omitting the second note and last note. This omission results in the notes which fall on the first and fourth beats becoming quarter notes. Most important melody notes occur on the first and fourth downbeat. As explained on page 43, these melody notes can be made more obvious by omitting the fill note that follows. Experiment with songs you know, omitting fill notes to emphasize the melody and avoid monotony.

HOME SWEET HOME

Music by Henry Bishop
Lyrics by John Payne

Arranged by Jack Hatfield

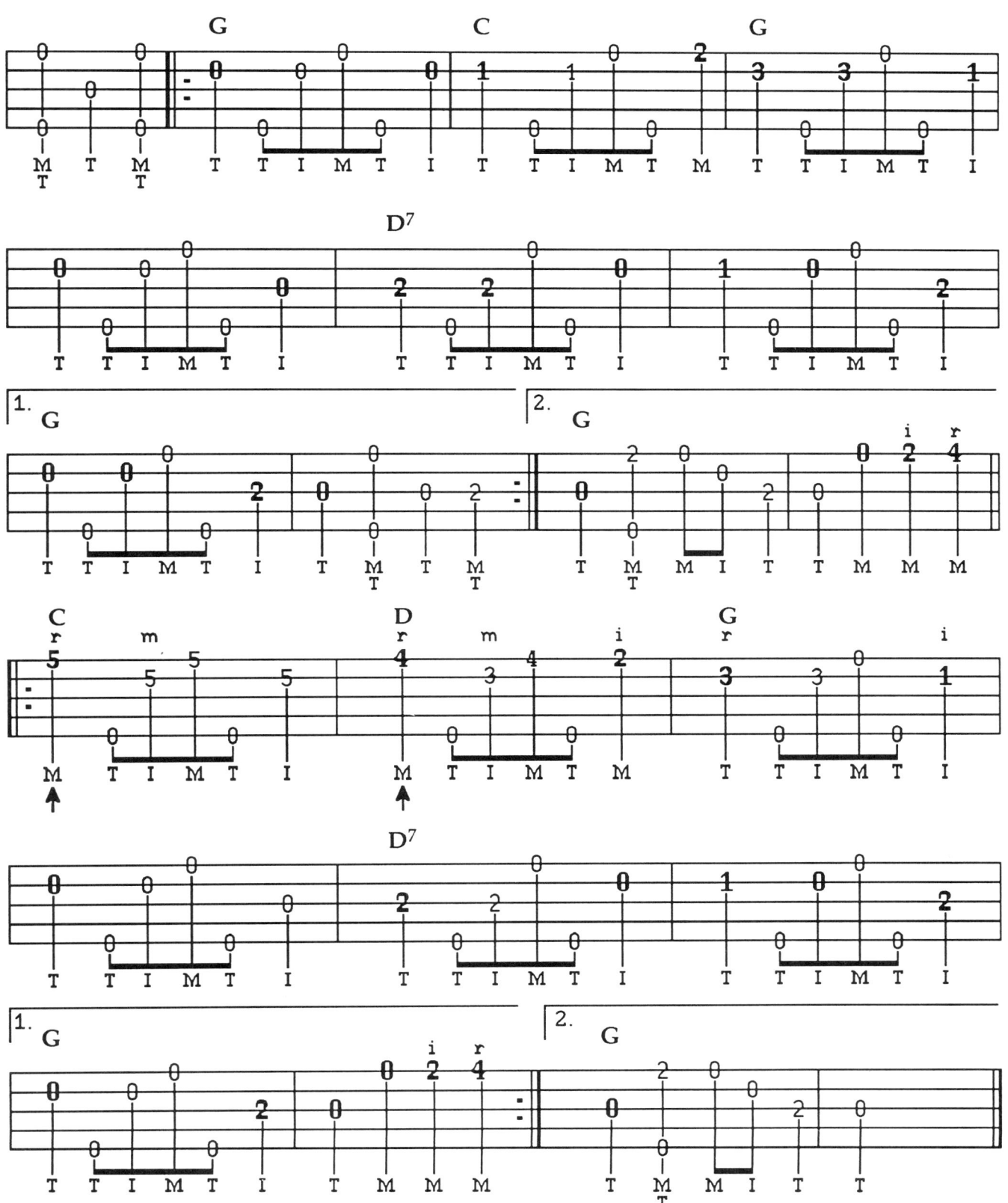

Note: The fourth line is difficult and should be practiced many times before starting on this song. The ring finger remains on the first string and the middle finger remains on the second string until the last note of measure two. Be sure to maintain string contact, sliding the fingertips from one position to the next.

LESSON 11

THE SLIDE

The <u>Slide</u> is a technique that draws attention to a melody note. Since the most important melody notes occur on the first beat of the measure, the most common note to slide is the first note of a roll.

To perform the slide, place your finger on a string, pick the string, and then slide the finger to another fret while the string is still vibrating. In tablature a slide will be shown as two numbers with a dash between them. The first number is the fret where the finger is placed to start the slide. The second number is the fret where the finger stops. Underneath the slide will be the letter *S*.

Most slides are from a lower fret <u>up</u> to a melody note.

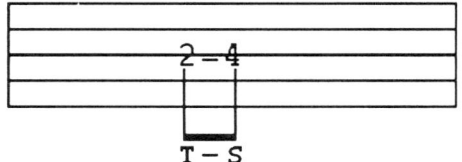

Slide from the 2nd to the 4th fret.

Practice the following exercise until the slide can be performed smoothly. <u>Do</u> <u>not</u> <u>break</u> <u>the</u> <u>right</u>-<u>hand</u> <u>rhythm</u>. All notes are equally spaced.

EXERCISE

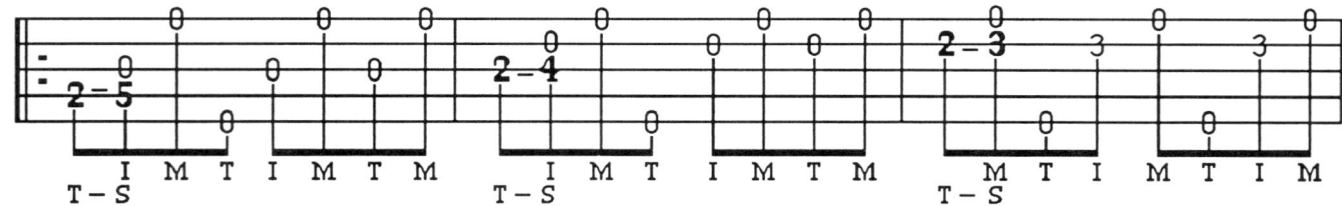

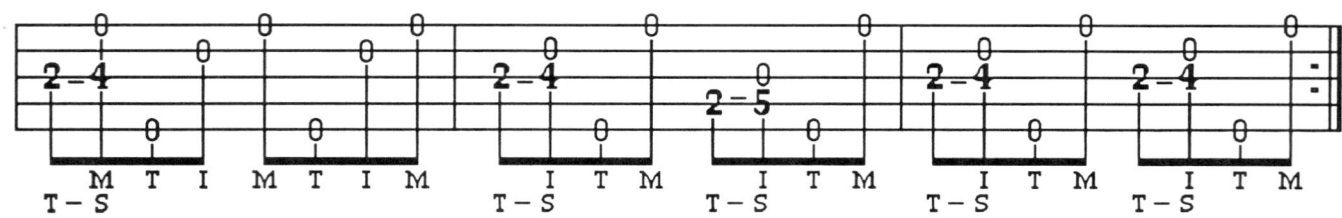

COMING 'ROUND THE MOUNTAIN

Traditional   Arranged by Jack Hatfield

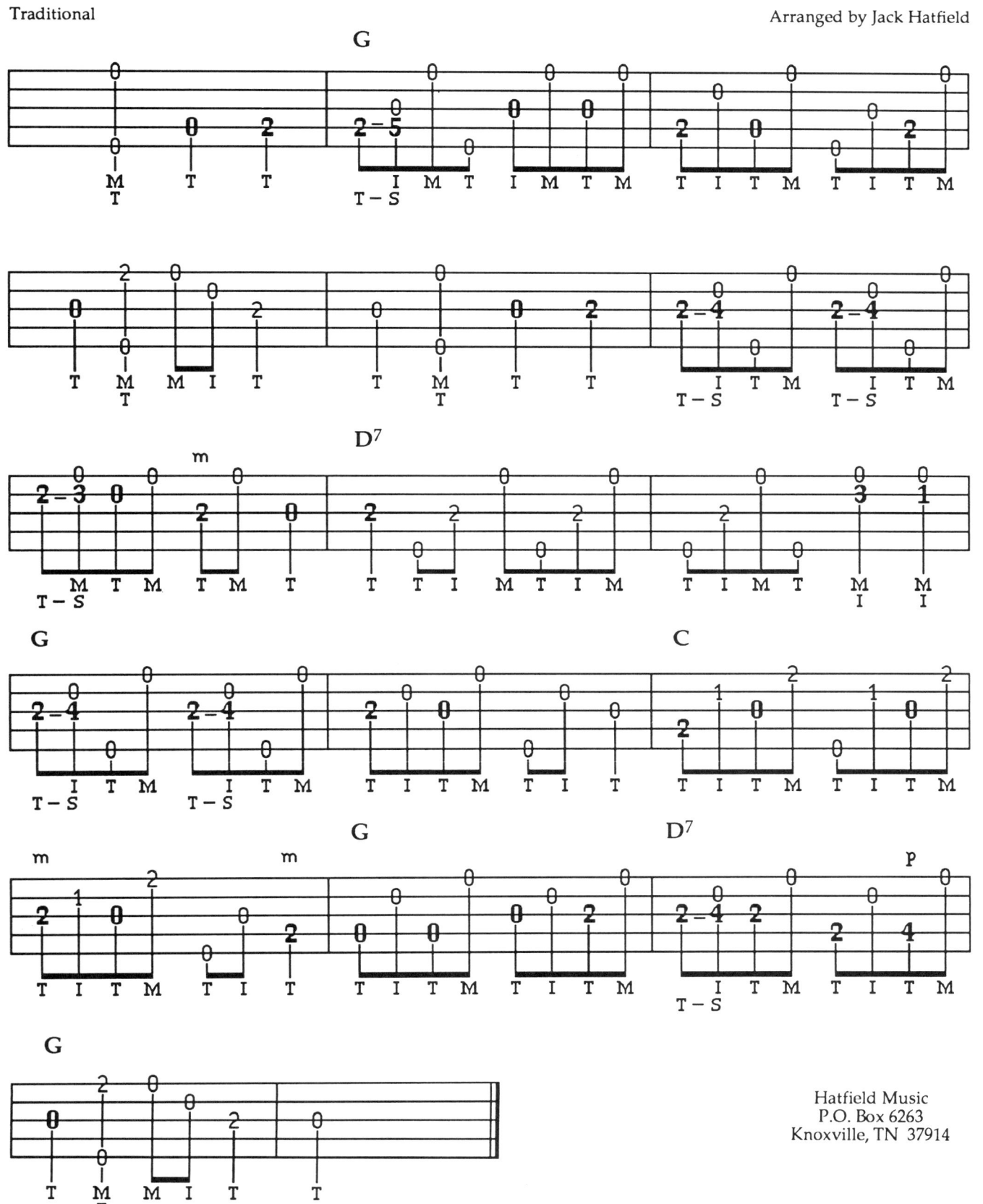

Hatfield Music
P.O. Box 6263
Knoxville, TN 37914

LESSON 12

TWO-MEASURE ROLLS

Music is often phrased in two-measure segments within a song. The following mixed rolls can be used in these situations:

TWO-MEASURE ROLL #1

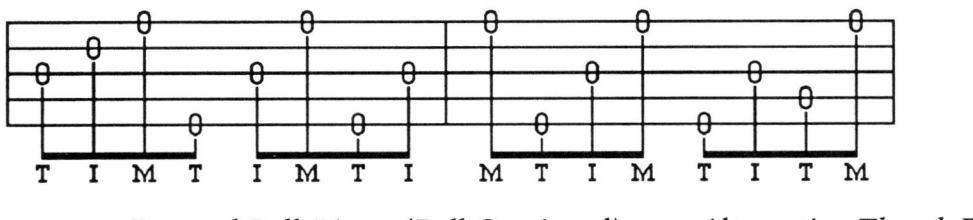

T I M T I M T I   M T I M T I T M

Forward Roll #1   (Roll Continued)   + Alternating Thumb Roll

TWO-MEASURE ROLL #2

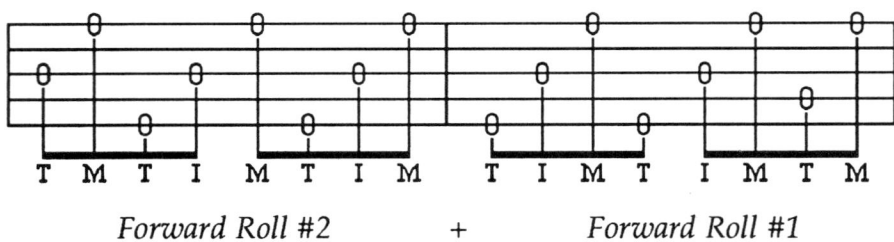

T M T I M T I M   T I M T I M T M

Forward Roll #2   +   Forward Roll #1

Practice both of these roll patterns until you can talk while performing them correctly, then proceed to <u>Banks of the Ohio</u> on the next page. This arrangement can be very tricky because in each two-measure roll different fill notes are omitted. Be very careful, especially in the all-important early stages of learning this song.

BANKS OF THE OHIO

Traditional
Arranged by Jack Hatfield

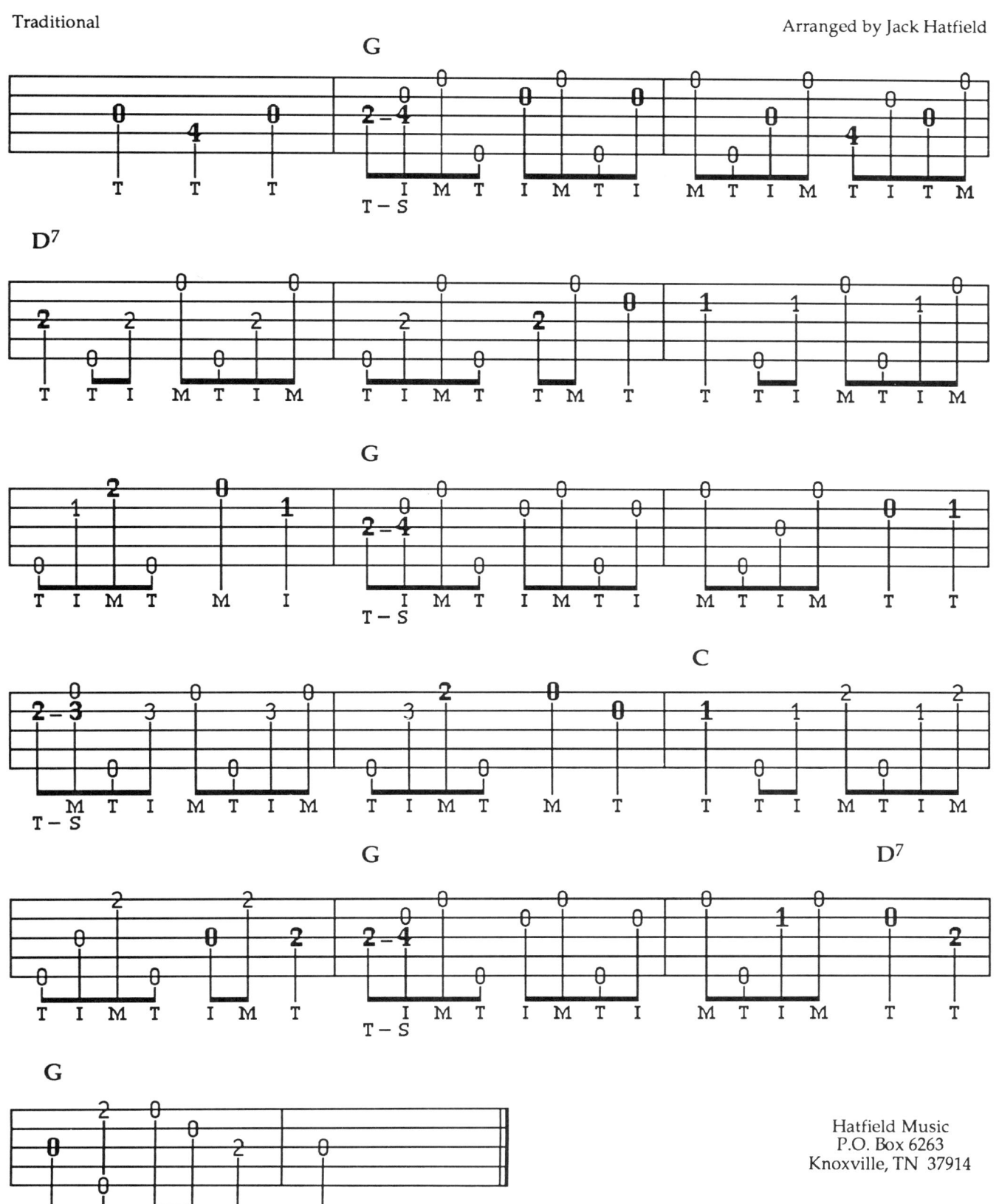

Hatfield Music
P.O. Box 6263
Knoxville, TN 37914

LESSON 13
THE REVERSE ROLL
(Also known as the *Forward - Backward Roll*)

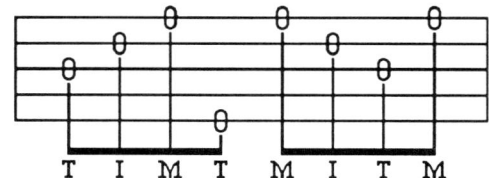

Practice this roll until it can be performed smoothly, then proceed to <u>Mountain</u> <u>Dew</u> on the following page.

NOTES:

MOUNTAIN DEW

Traditional   Arranged by Jack Hatfield

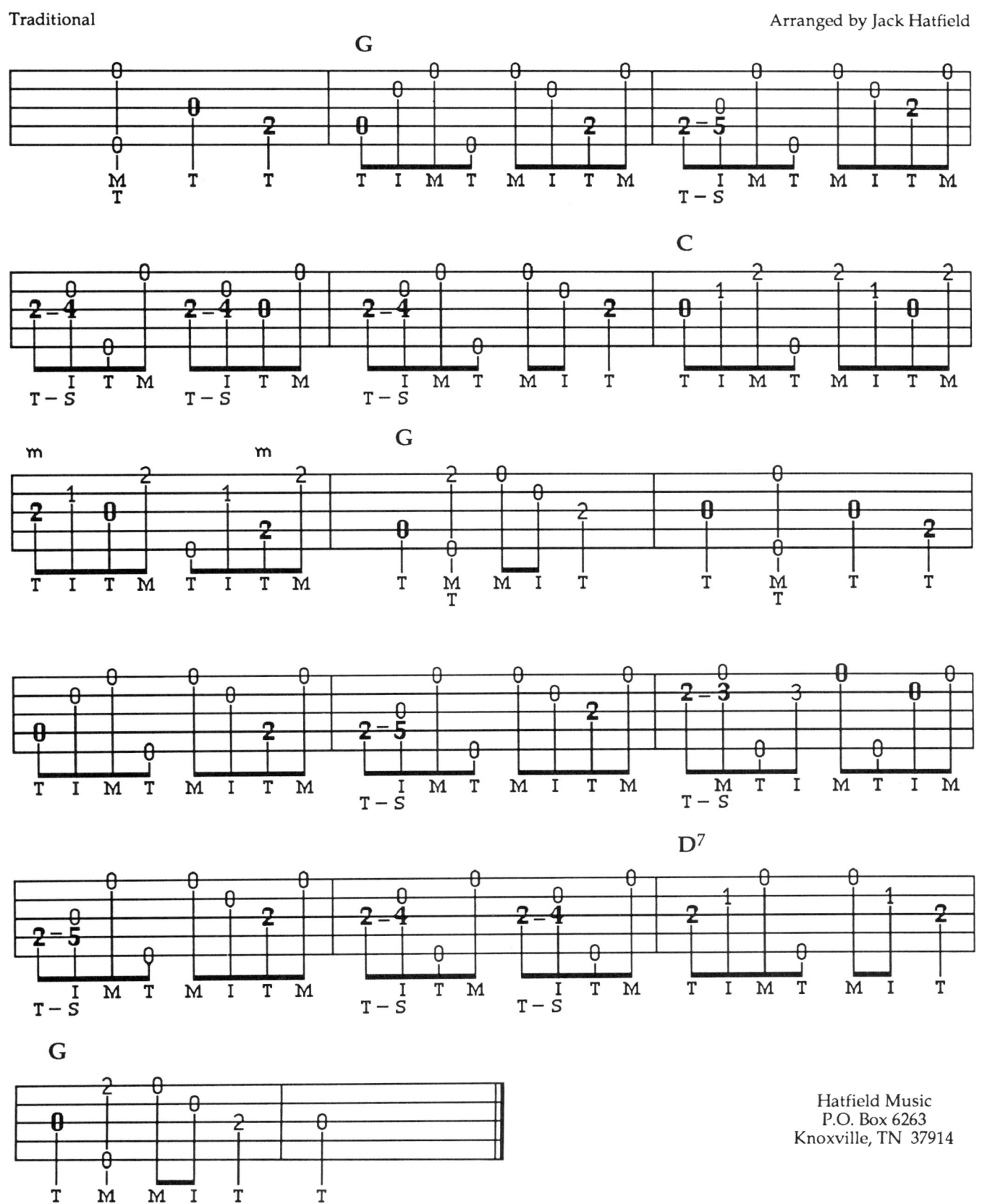

Hatfield Music
P.O. Box 6263
Knoxville, TN 37914

LESSON 14

THE HAMMER-ON

The Hammer-On is another left-hand technique. Like the slide, it draws attention to melody notes. It can also be used strictly for embellishment. A Hammer-On can be done on an open string or a fretted string. Here is what the Hammer-On looks like in tablature:

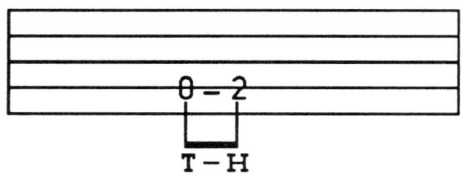 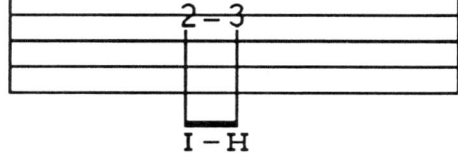

Hammer-On from an open string.   *Hammer-On from a fretted string.*

The letter *H* underneath a note helps to distinguish the hammer-on from the slide (which has the letter *S* underneath). To perform the first example presented above:

a) Pick the open fourth string with the Thumb.

b) While the string is still vibrating, immediately snap the middle finger of the left hand down behind the second fret.

This produces two notes in quick succession even though the right hand only picked the string once.

To perform the second example shown above:

a) Place the index finger of the left hand on the second string, second fret.

b) Pick the second string with the Index finger of the right hand.

c) Immediately snap the middle (or ring) finger of the left hand down behind the third fret while the string is still vibrating.

The arrangement which follows uses some common hammers-on. It also mixes many of the rolls learned previously.

BURY ME BENEATH THE WILLOW

Traditional   Arranged by Jack Hatfield

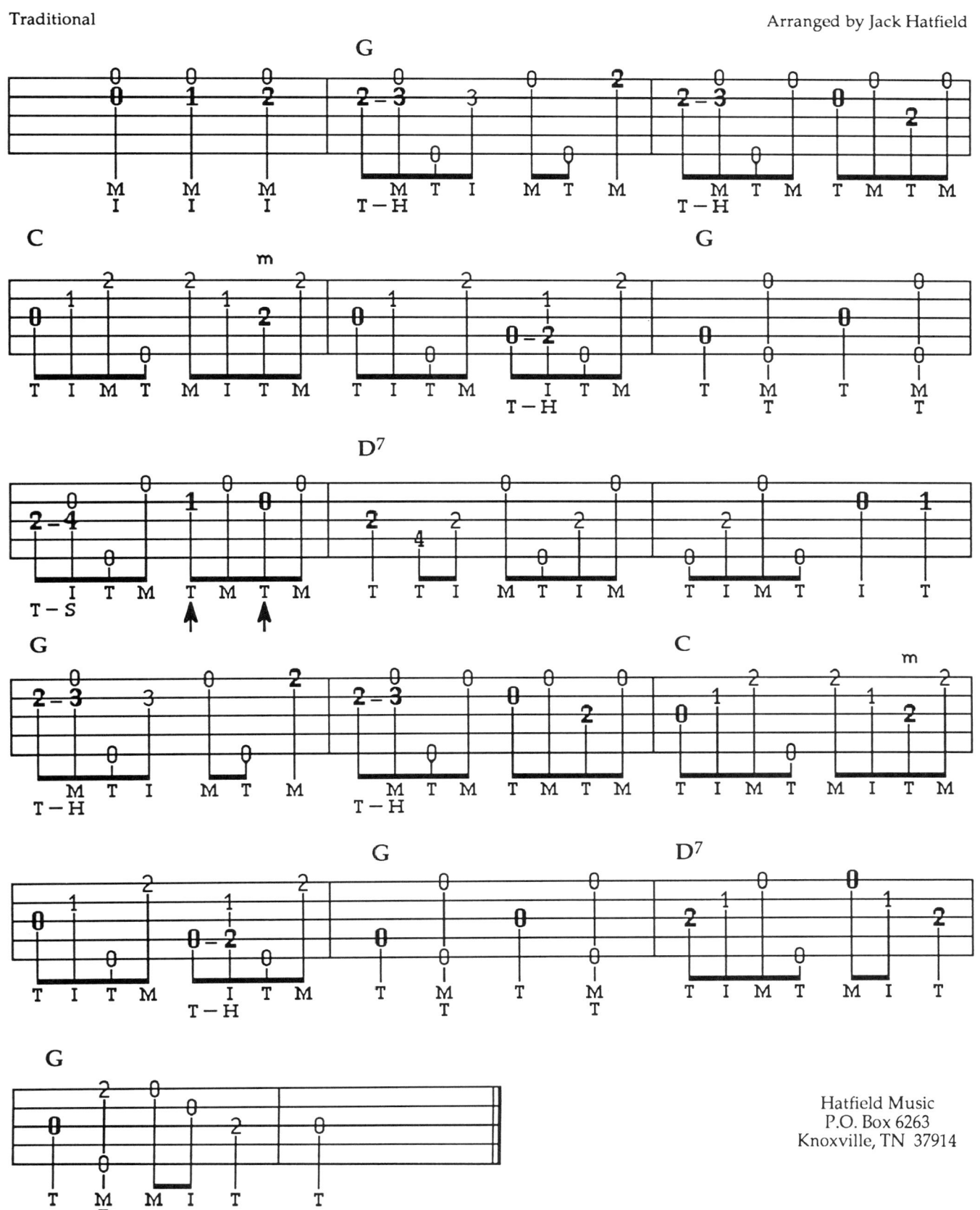

Hatfield Music
P.O. Box 6263
Knoxville, TN 37914

LESSON 15

THE PULL-OFF

The Pull-Off is a left-hand technique that can be thought of as a backwards hammer-on. Like the slide and the hammer-on, it is used for emphasis. More often than other left-hand techniques, it is used simply for embellishment.

Here is what the Pull-Off looks like in tablature:

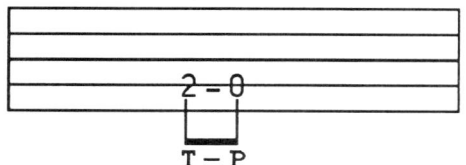   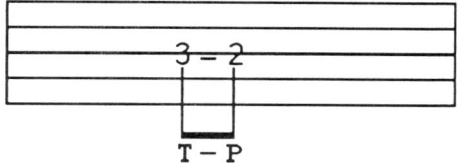

Pull-Off to an open string.   *Pull-Off to a fretted string.*

The letter *P* underneath a note helps to establish the pull-off from the slide and hammer-on. Remember, a pull-off goes from a fretted note to an open string or to a lower fretted note, whereas a hammer-on goes to a higher fret. A slide can go in an upward or downward direction, although downward slides are rare. To perform the first example presented above:

a) Place the middle finger on the fourth string, second fret.

b) Pick the string with the thumb of the right hand.

c) While the string is still vibrating, pull the middle finger off the string quickly with a sideways motion as if picking the string with the left hand.

To perform the second example shown above:

a) Place the middle (or ring) finger of the left hand on the third string, third fret.

b) Simultaneously place the index finger of the left hand on the third string, second fret.

c) Pick the third string with the Thumb of the right hand.

d) While the string is still vibrating, snap the third fret finger off the string as described in (c) above.

e) Leave the index finger down for a brief instant after the pull-off has been performed.

PULL-OFF EXERCISES

EXERCISE 1

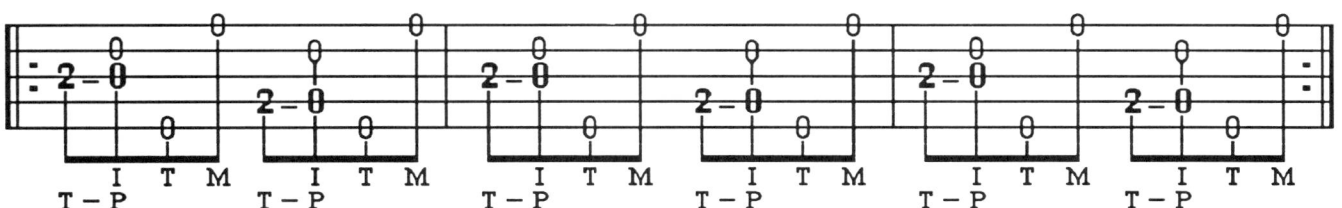

EXERCISE 2

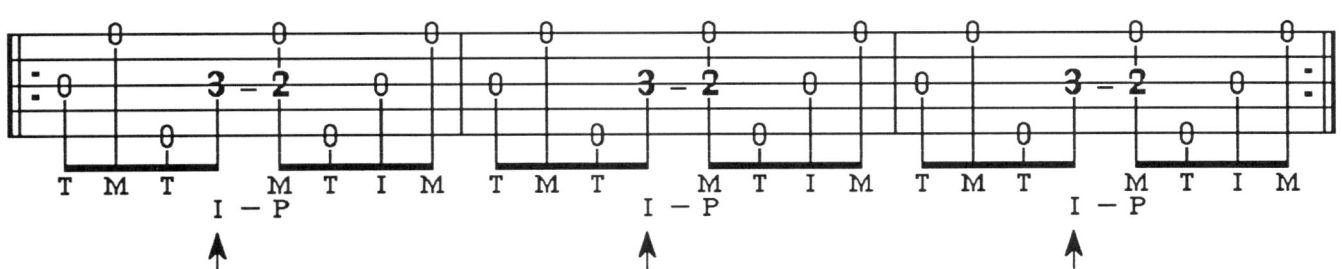

EXERCISE 3

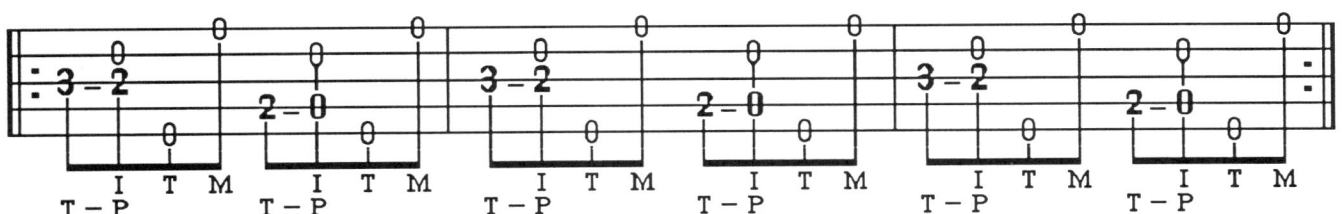

<u>Cripple</u> <u>Creek</u> on the following page is a much-loved banjo tune. It employs the popular 2 - 0 pull-off.

CRIPPLE CREEK

Traditional Arranged by Jack Hatfield

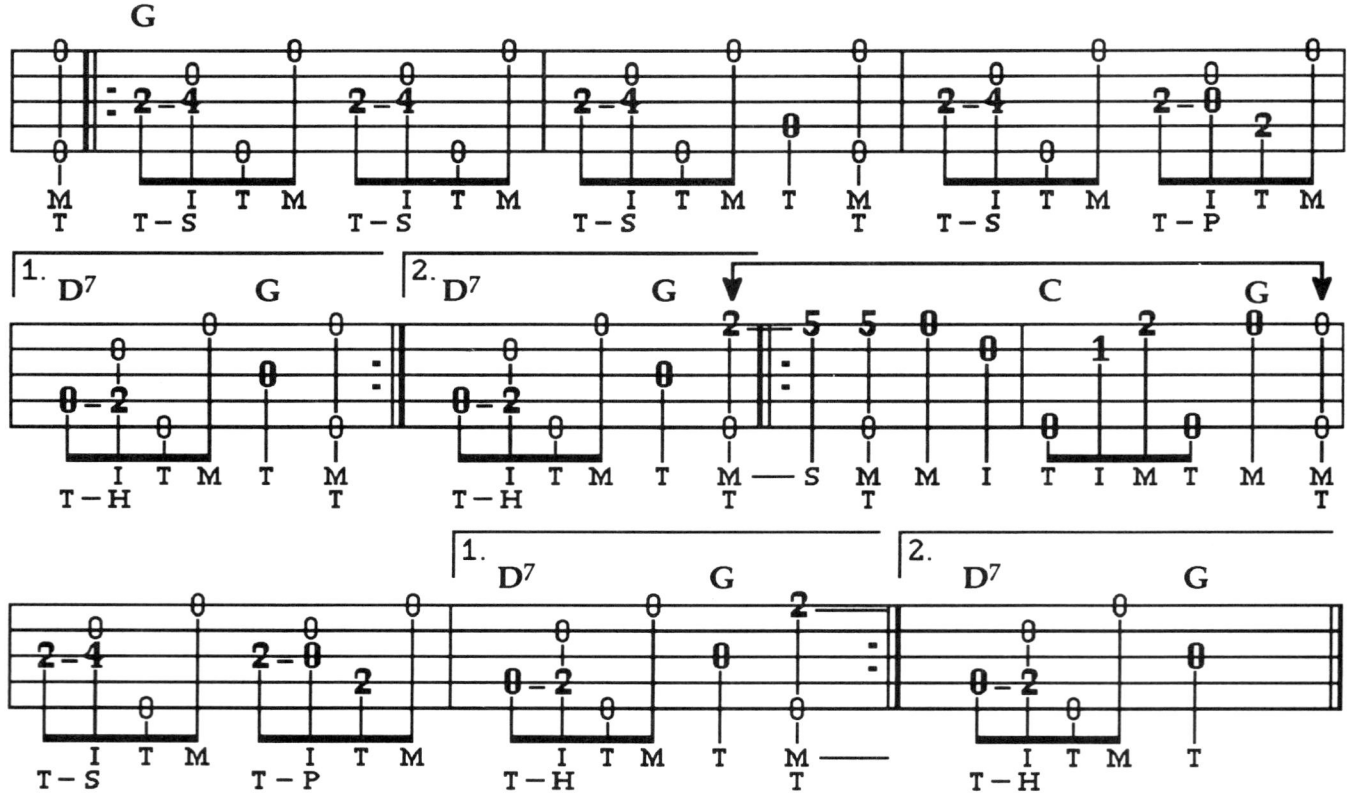

Note: *The area marked by the caution arrows is a tricky spot in regard to timing. When doing the 2 - 5 slide, note that both the 2 and the 5 are quarter notes, so the entire slide consumes two beats - twice as long as previous slides. Also, be careful not to rush the note that occupies the fourth beat of that measure.*

NOTES:

LESSON 16
THE REVERSE ROLL #2
(The *Tag Roll*)

The following pattern is the Tag Roll. As the name implies, it is often used to end a phrase. Learn this roll and its varitations which are formed by omitting fill notes as previously discussed.

REVERSE ROLL #2 (*Tag Roll*)

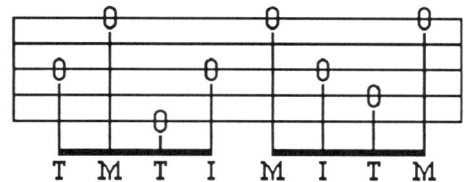

VARIATION #1

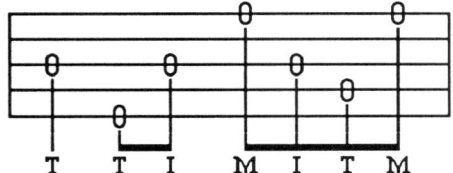

VARIATION #2

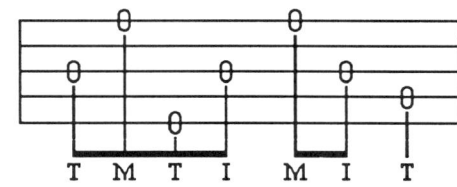

VARIATION #3

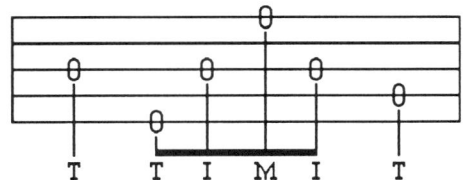

THE TAG LICK

The <u>Tag Lick</u> is probably the most-used lick in bluegrass banjo playing. Below are some examples of the Tag Lick using the variations of the tag roll shown on the previous page along with various hammers-on and pulls-off.

#1

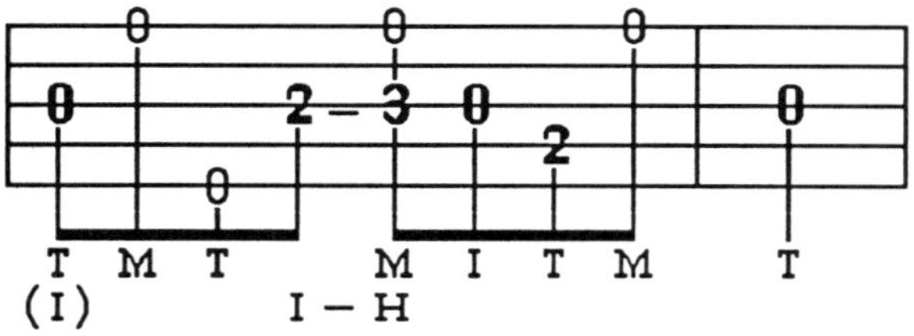

#2

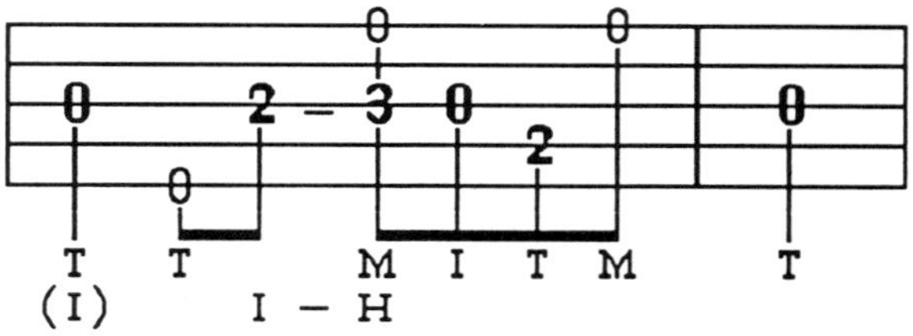

#3

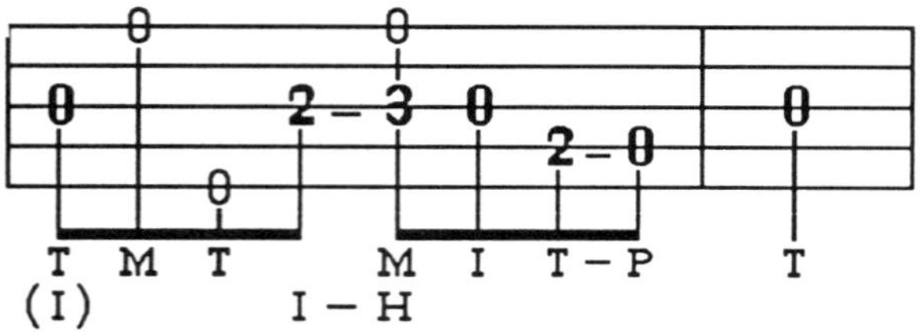

#4

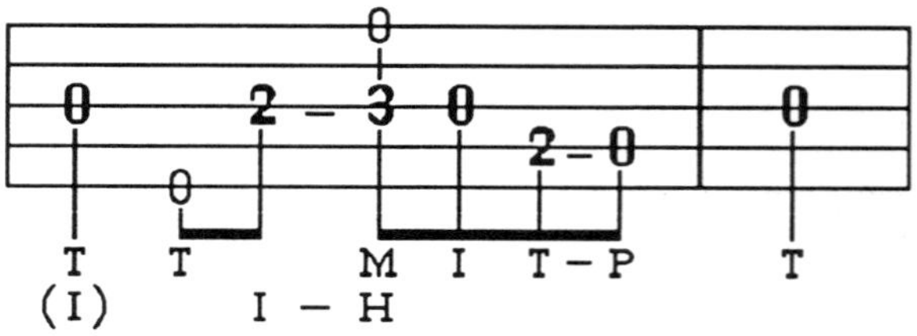

#5

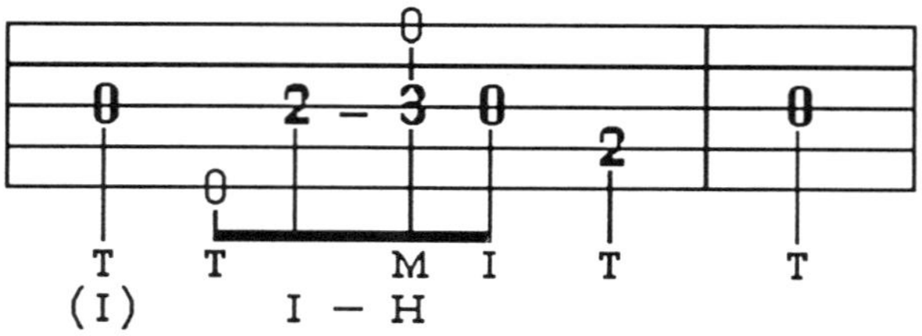

The arrangement on the following page makes frequent use of the Tag Roll and ends with the Tag Lick, as many songs will from this point forward.

OLD TIME RELIGION

Traditional Arranged by Jack Hatfield

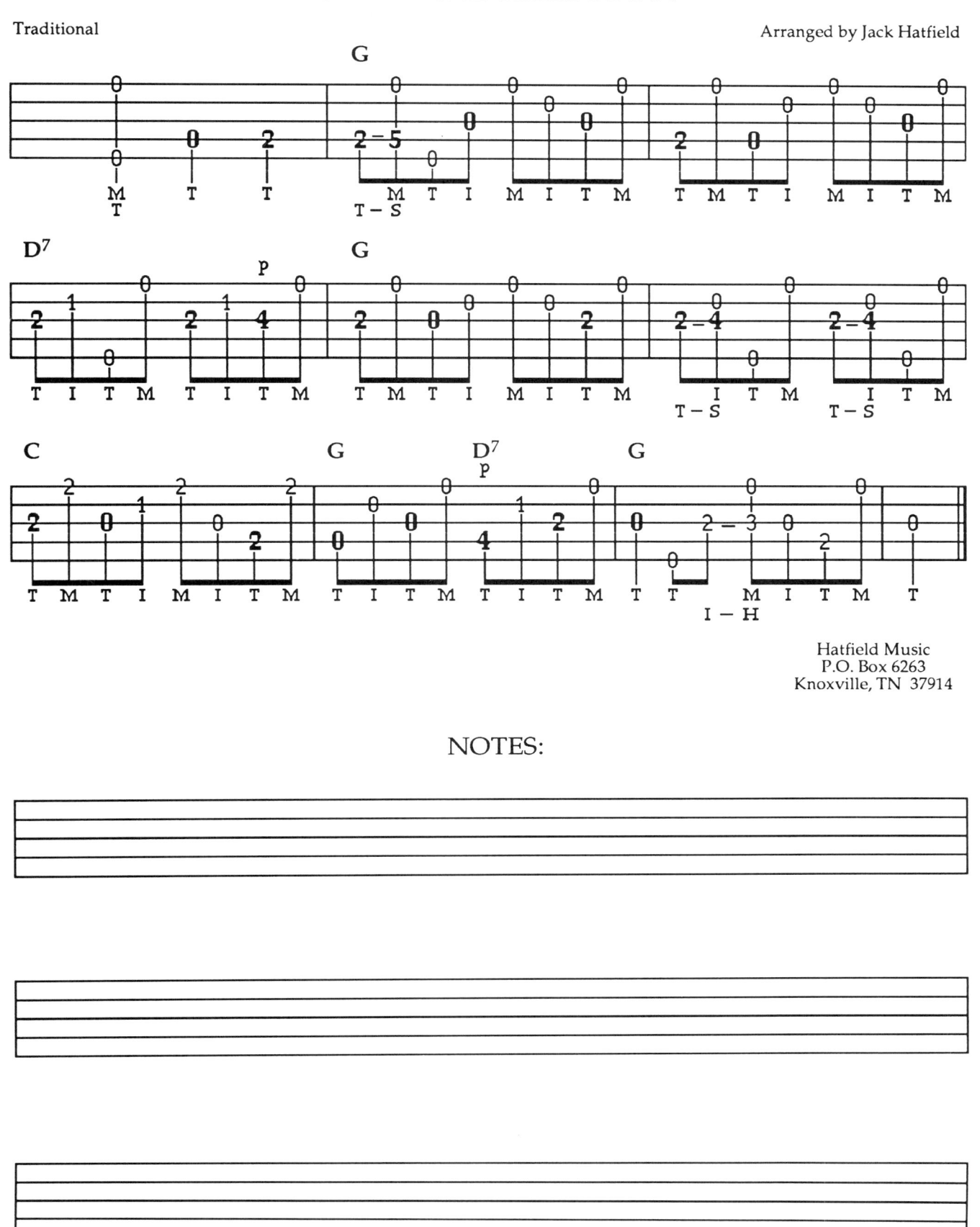

Hatfield Music
P.O. Box 6263
Knoxville, TN 37914

NOTES:

63

LESSON 17

THE FOGGY MOUNTAIN ROLL

Below is the Foggy Mountain Roll, so named because it is the opening roll for *Foggy Mountain Breakdown*, Earl Scrugg's masterpiece and probably the most famous of all bluegrass banjo songs.

THE FOGGY MOUNTAIN ROLL

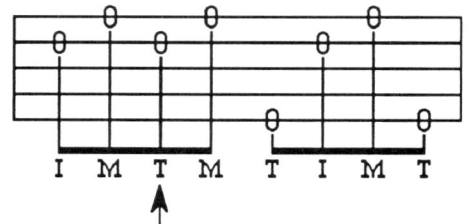

The Foggy Mountain Roll is often performed in conjunction with hammers-on. Be sure to use the Thumb on the third note of the roll (not the Index) when practicing the following exercise:

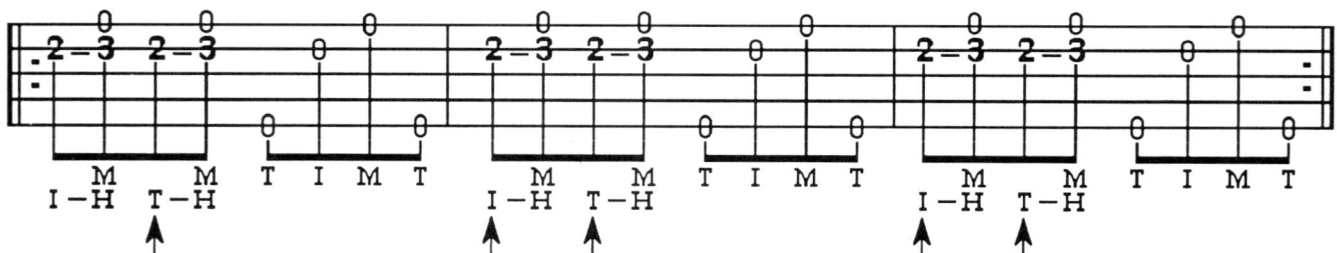

Notice that this roll ends with the Thumb. Since this ending note is also an eighth note, you will not have time to start the next roll with the Thumb. At performing speed there simply is not enough time to use the same right-hand finger twice in a row if the first of the two notes is an eighth note. This is one of the few rules in three-finger style banjo playing to which there are No Exceptions. This means that when using the Foggy Mountain Roll, you will have to alter the next roll to start with the Index or Middle finger (usually Index).

An arrow (↑) marks the places where you will have to alter your right-hand fingering in the arrangement of Train '45 on the following page. BE CAREFUL!

TRAIN '45

Traditional
Arranged by Jack Hatfield

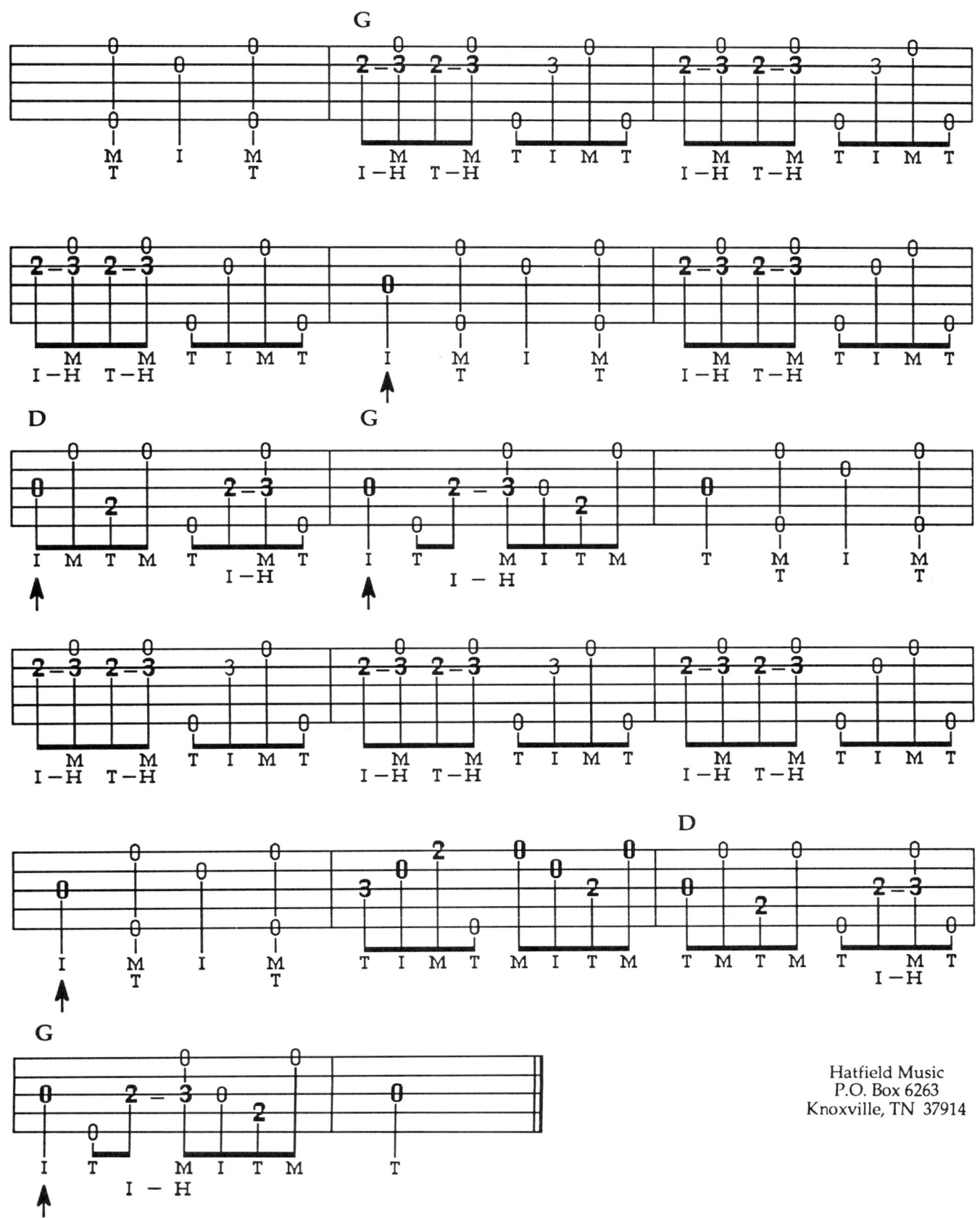

Hatfield Music
P.O. Box 6263
Knoxville, TN 37914

LESSON 18

THE ALTERNATING MIDDLE ROLL

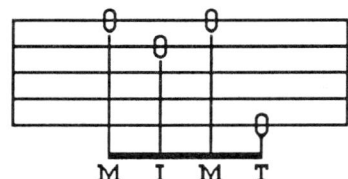

This roll is often used when the melody occurs on the first string, as it does in the song below.

OLD JOE CLARK

Traditional   Arranged by Jack Hatfield

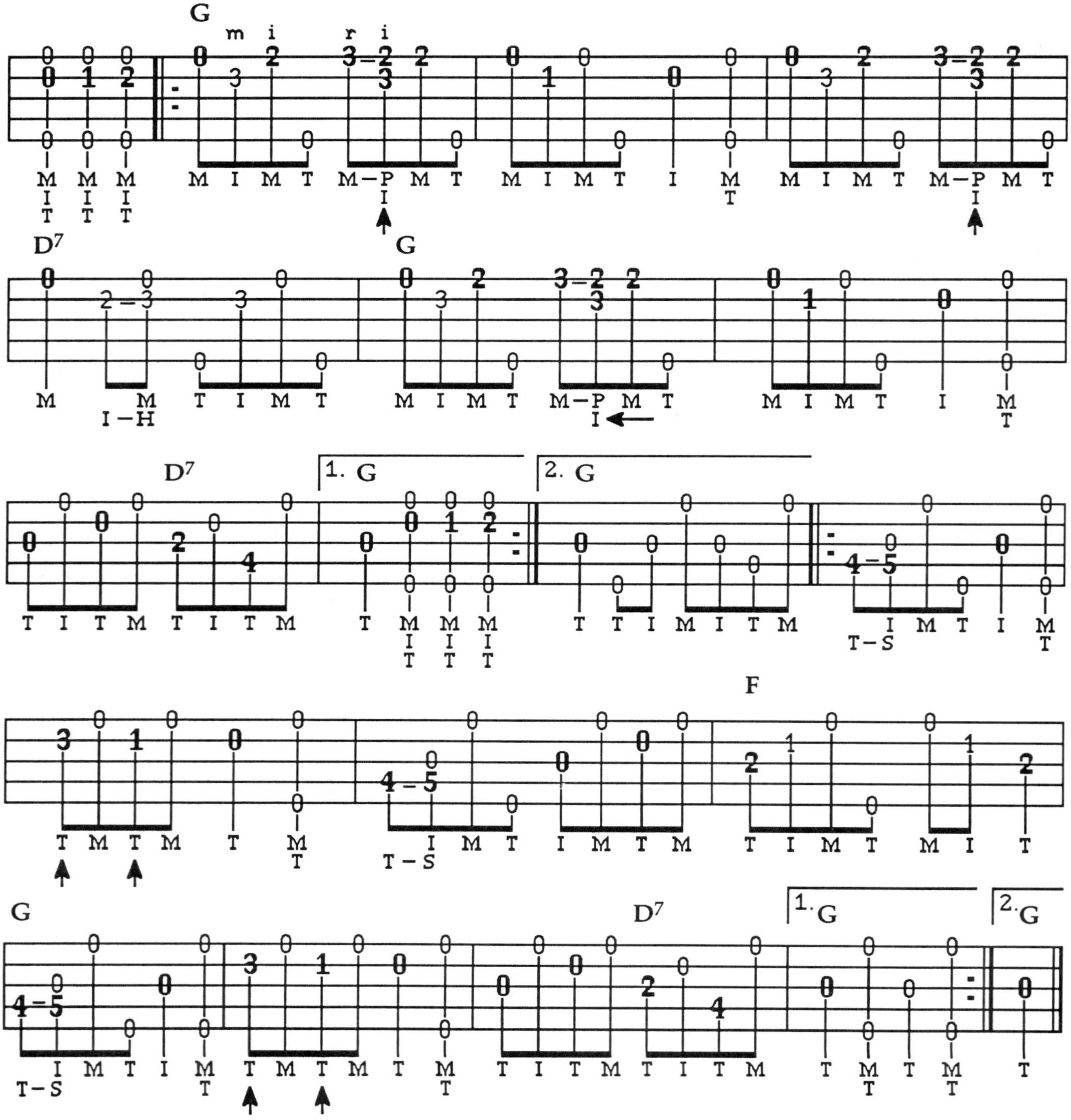

LESSON 19

THE BACKWARD ROLL

The Backward Roll is not as clearly defined as the other rolls, possibly because it has not been found to be as useful. Any pattern that contains more than one M I T sequence within the measure can be considered a Backward Roll. The following are some examples:

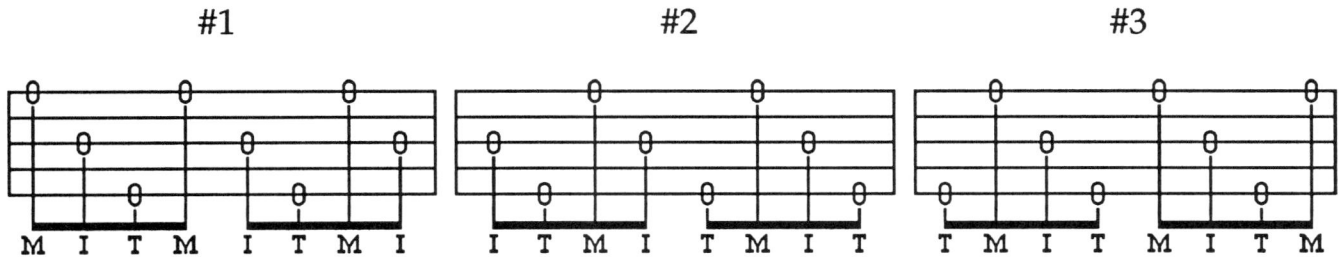

A Backward Roll repeated over and over at a moderate tempo can produce a syncopated (bouncy or unevenly accented) rhythm.

HANDSOME MOLLY

Traditional

Arranged by Jack Hatfield

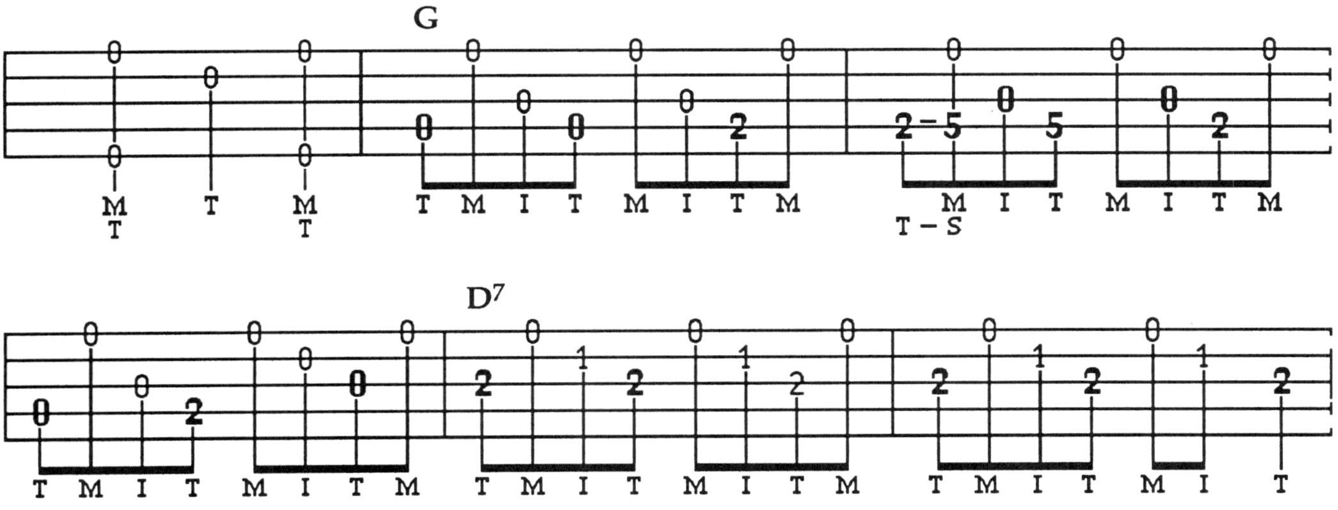

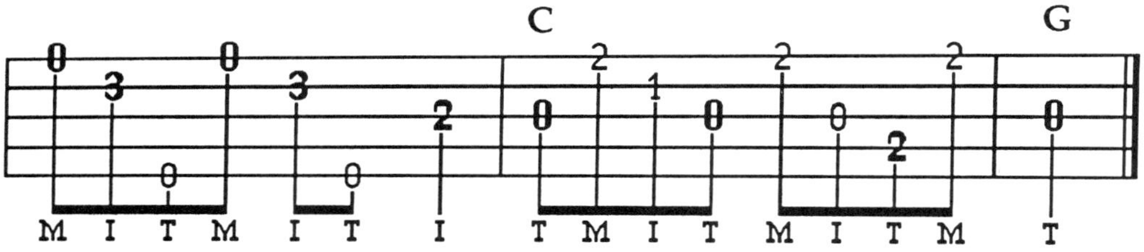

Hatfield Music
P.O. Box 6263
Knoxville, TN 37914

LESSON 20

THE BACKWARD-FORWARD ROLL

The <u>Backward</u>-<u>Forward</u> Roll is another roll used in those rare occasions when the melody note is found on the first string. The first string notes are usually accented (*). This produces a *loping* rhythm. Striking the fifth string notes more lightly will also help you achieve this effect.

THE BACKWARD-FORWARD ROLL

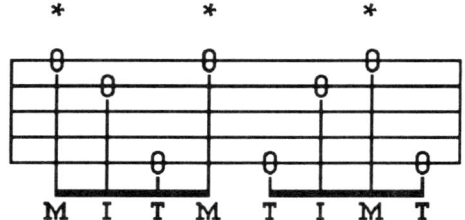

Now learn <u>John Henry</u> on the following page. Be sure to observe the left-hand fingerings above the notes. Leave the middle finger of the left hand down constantly on the second string, third fret throughout the first three lines. The only exceptions are for the third from last note in the first line and the first measure of the second line. Like the Foggy Mountain Roll, this pattern ends with the Thumb, so you will not be able to start the next roll with the Thumb.

JOHN HENRY

Traditional
Arranged by Jack Hatfield

BASIC CHORD FORMATIONS

Some new chords will be introduced in the arrangements which follow. The chord symbols will be shown above the tablature as they have been throughout the book. The entire chord will not always be held - only one or two of the chord tones may actually be sounded or a note may be added to the chord as dictated by the melody of the song. By now you should have realized that holding the appropriate left-hand formations makes playing most songs immensely easier and more efficient.

To get a better understanding of how the chord progression relates to the melody, it would be a good idea to strum through the progression before learning the song while singing or humming the melody if it is familiar to you. If it is not, then listen to the cassette tape that accompanies this book until you know the melody. Learning time can be cut in half if the melody is already familiar to you before you start practicing the tune.

PLAYING WITH A RHYTHM GUITARIST

Playing with a rhythm guitarist would be helpful at this point. If a rhythm guitarist is available, practice with him as often as possible. He not only fills out the total sound, but also helps you keep a steady beat. He will force you to recognize and correct timing mistakes you may inadvertently be making, such as *stuttering* (going back to pick up missed notes). This is common among novice pickers and can be disastrous. Besides all of this, it is simply a lot more fun to play with others. The guitar player should play the following simple alternating bass note rhythm pattern:

        1st Beat - Root bass note
        2nd Beat - Strum
        3rd Beat - Alternate bass note
        4th Beat - Strum

LESSON 21

THE D CHORD

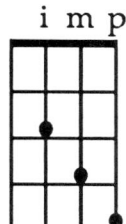

Be sure to use the pinky, not the ring finger, on the first string.

WILL THE CIRCLE BE UNBROKEN

Traditional
Arranged by Jack Hatfield

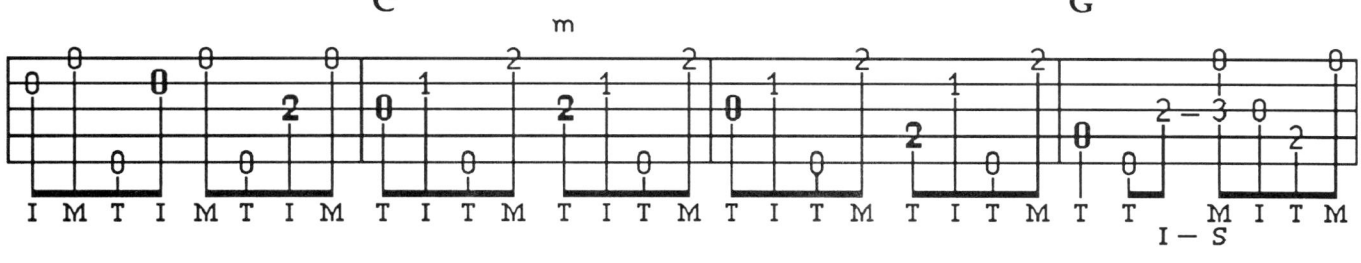
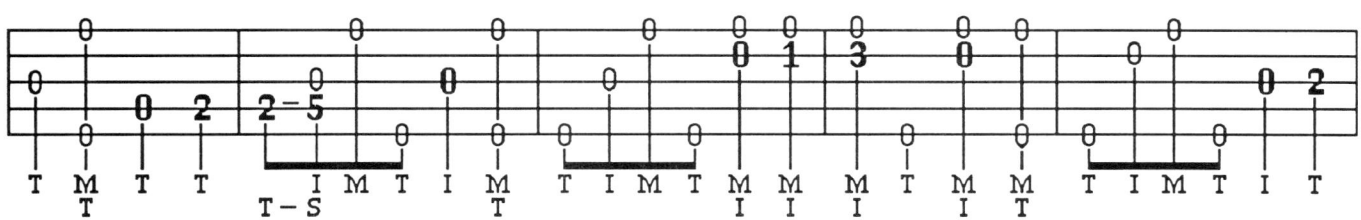
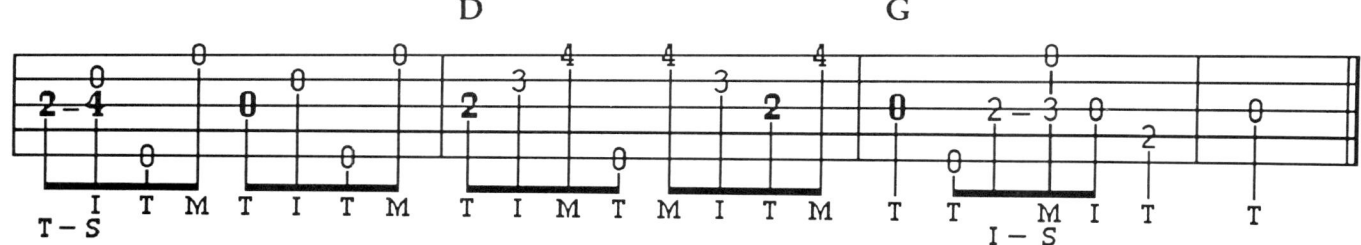

LESSON 22

ANOTHER D FORMATION

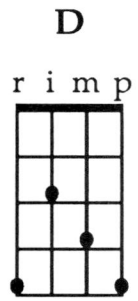

This is one of the three basic Major chord forms and should be memorized. The chord progression to <u>D Banjo Boogie</u> is called a *Twelve Bar Blues* and is probably the most commonly used progression in popular music. It is written in the key of D in which the three principle chords are **D**, **G**, and **A**. Up to this point, you have played everything in the key of G where the principle chords are **G**, **C**, and **D**. To play this arrangement in the key of G, move everything up 5 frets, using a **G** to replace **D**, **C** to replace **G**, and **D** to replace **A**.

D BANJO BOOGIE

Jack Hatfield

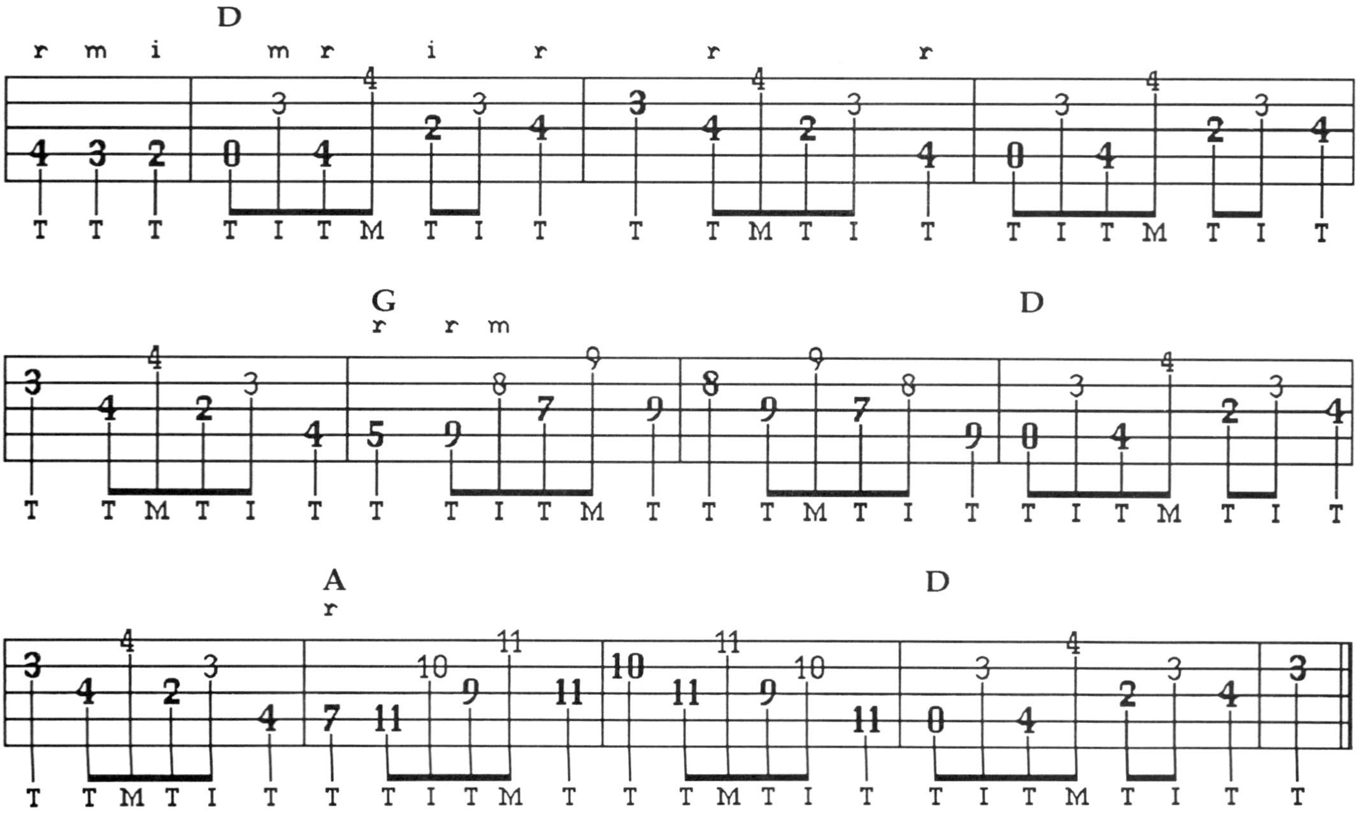

LESSON 23

THE E minor AND A minor CHORDS

Em
m   r

Am
x m i r

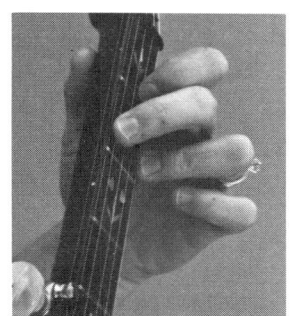

SAIL AWAY LADIES

Traditional

Arranged by Jack Hatfield

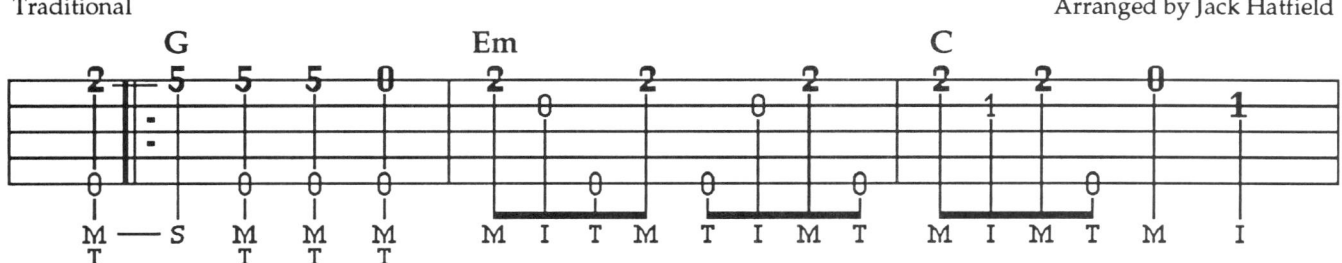
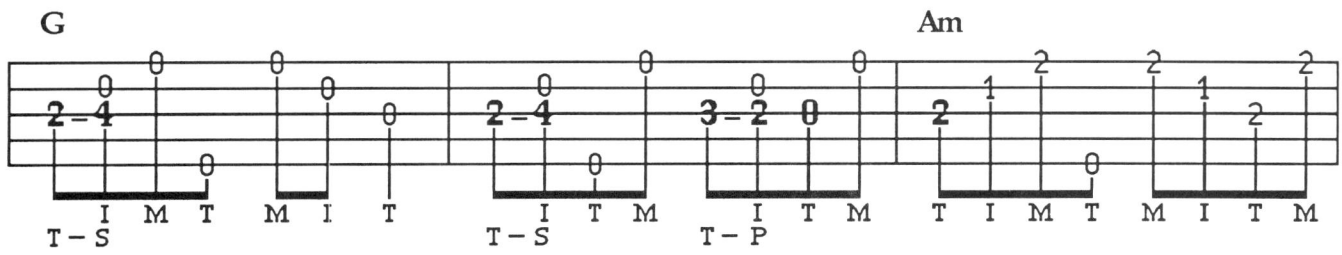
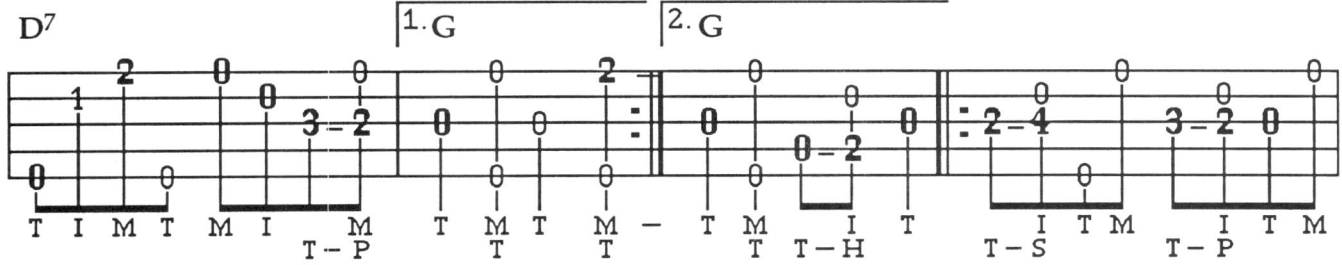
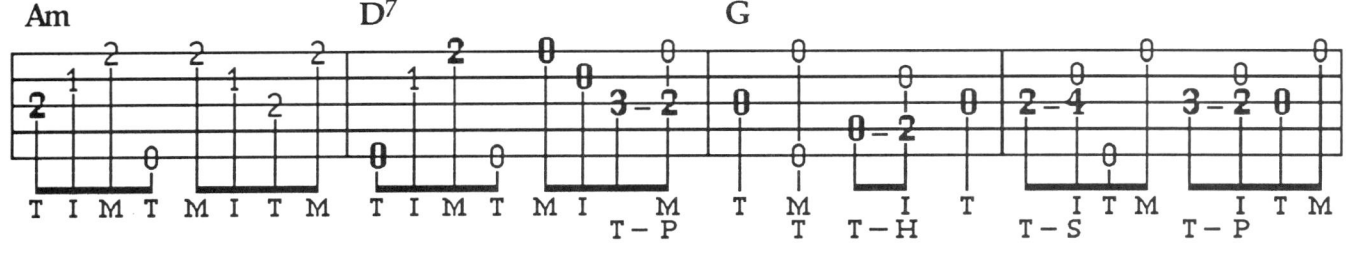
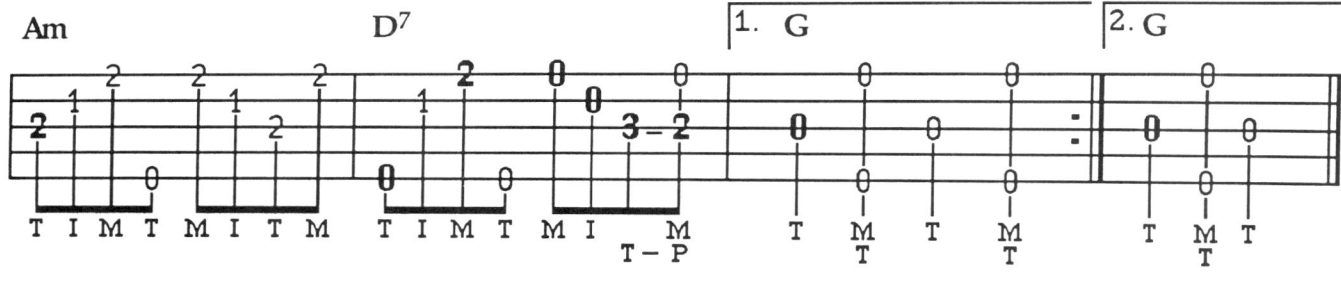

LESSON 24
THE F CHORD

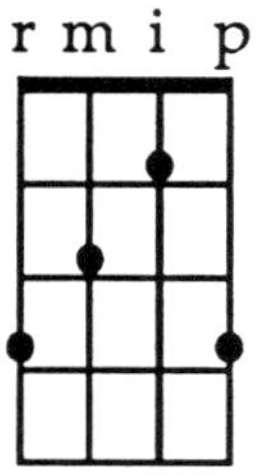

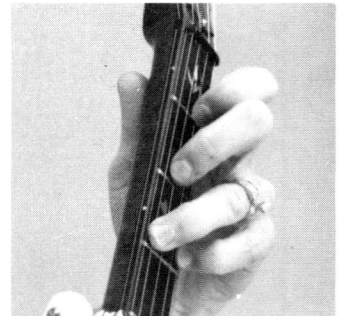

This is another one of the three basic Major chord forms which should be memorized. The other Major forms that can be made on the banjo in G tuning are the D formation on page 72 and the Bar formation on page 75.

LITTLE MAGGIE

Traditional   Arranged by Jack Hatfield

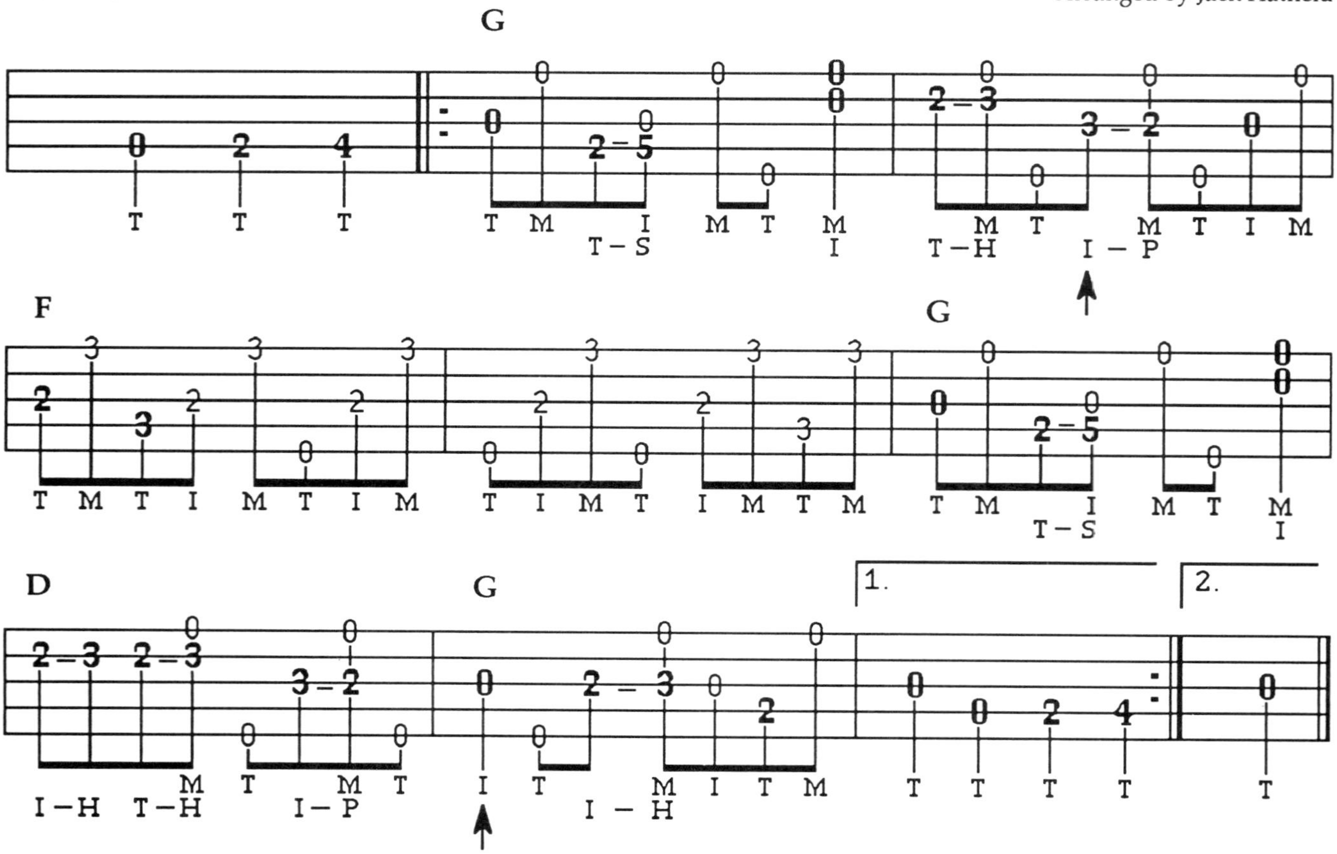

Hatfield Music
P.O. Box 6263
Knoxville, TN 37914

LESSON 25

THE A AND B7 CHORDS

A

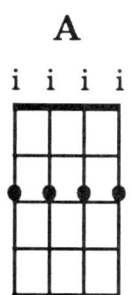 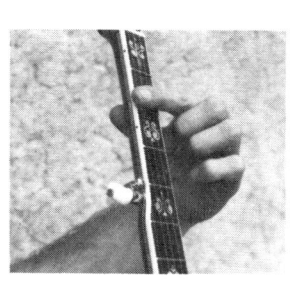

B7

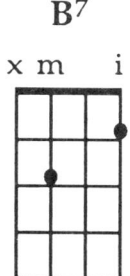 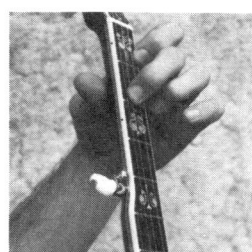

The **A** is a <u>Bar</u> chord, meaning one finger is held across all of the strings at the same fret. The Bar formation is the last of the three basic Major chord formations.

MAKE ME A PALLET ON YOUR FLOOR

Traditional

Arranged by Jack Hatfield

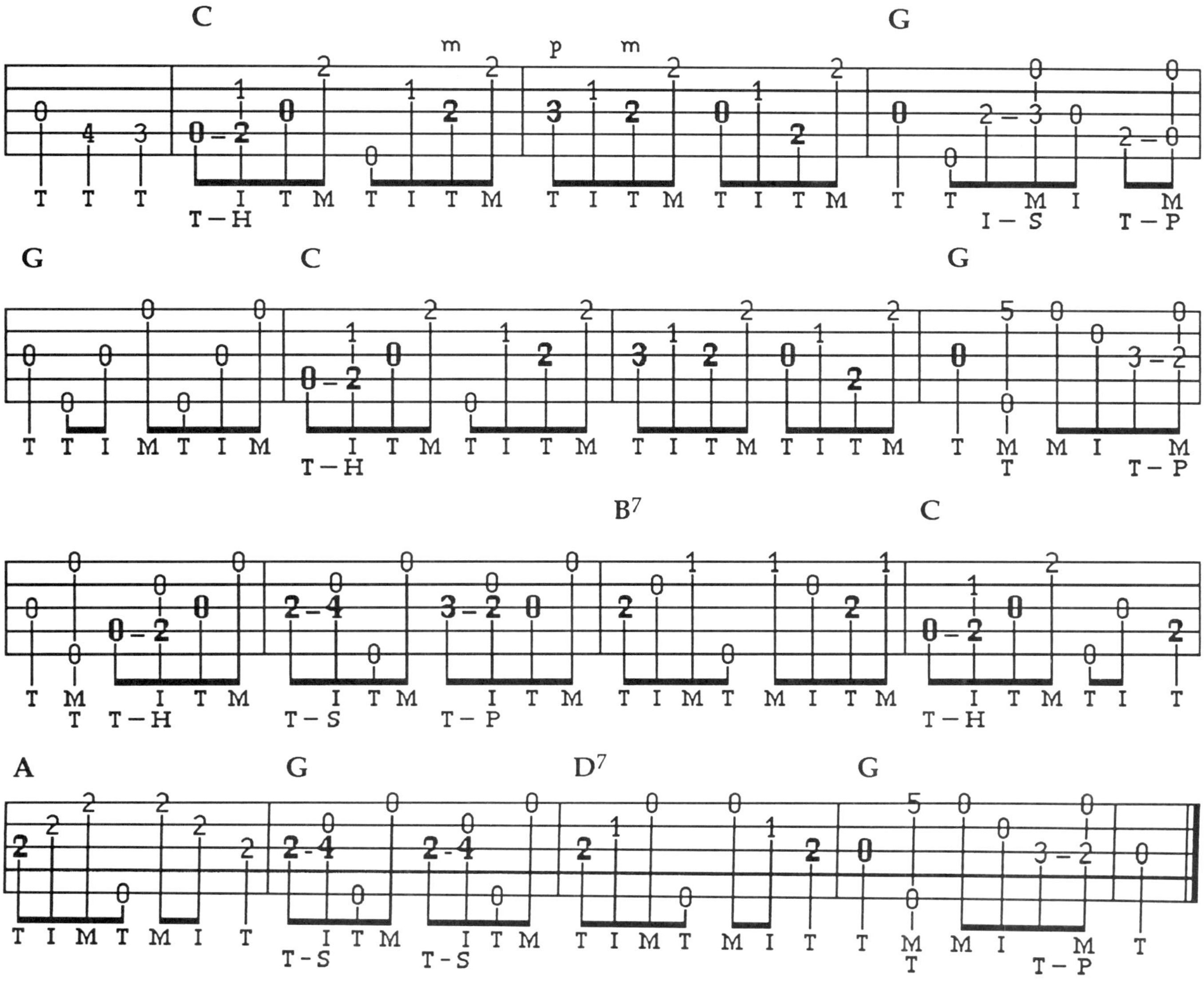

CHORD - ROLL EXERCISES

These exercises are designed to facilitate faster chord changing, smoother rolls, and better coordination of the right and left hands. Play each exercise continuously for several minutes daily. Do not pause when repeating.

EXERCISE #1

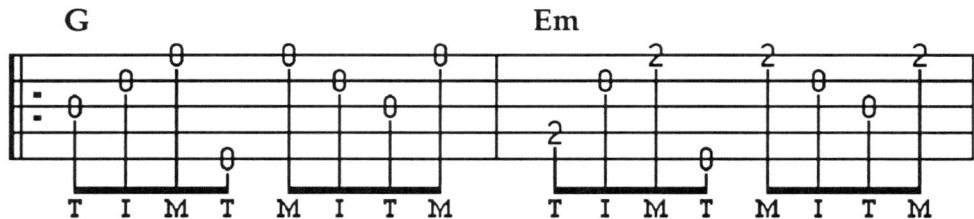

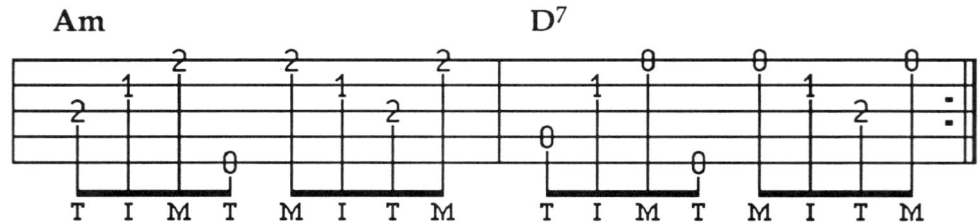

EXERCISE #2

Note: Often a fill note just before a chord change is played open, giving the left hand a "head start" on the upcoming difficult maneuver.

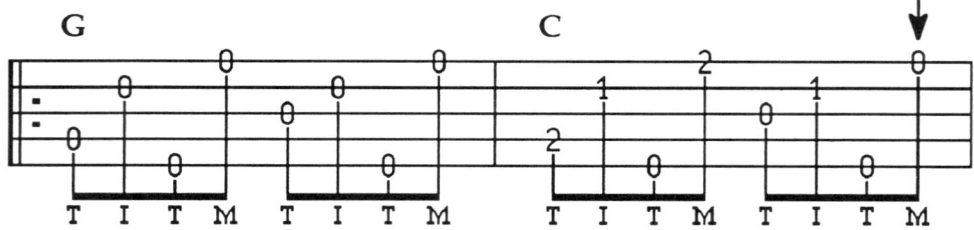

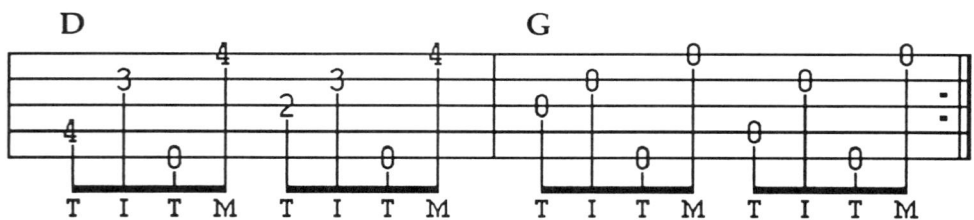

EXERCISE #3

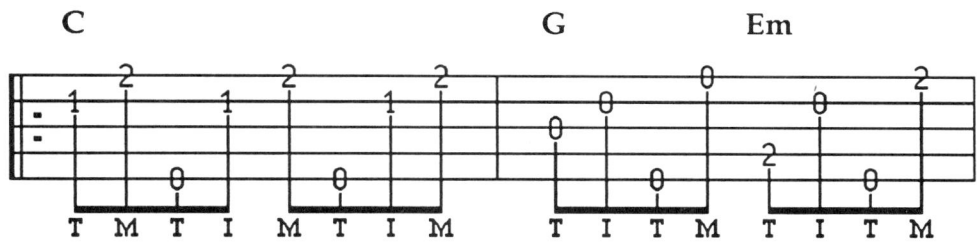

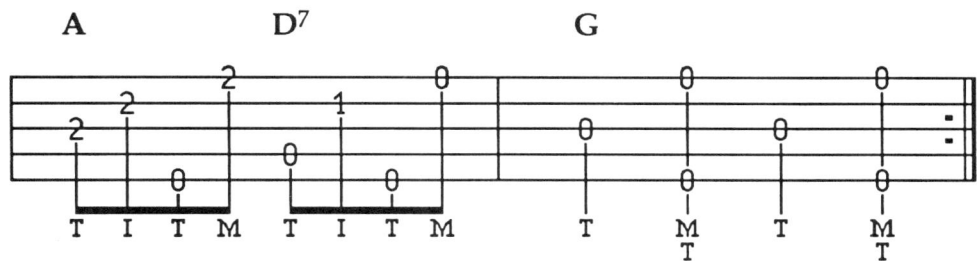

EXERCISE #4

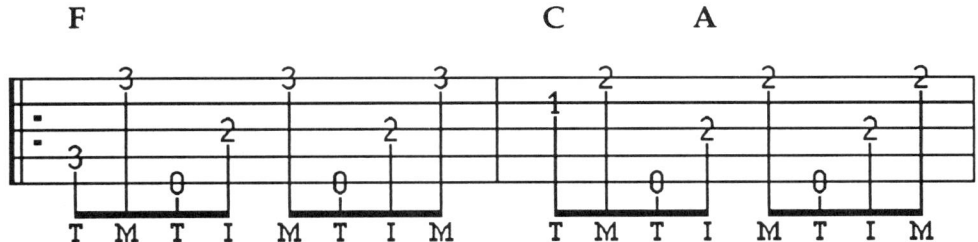

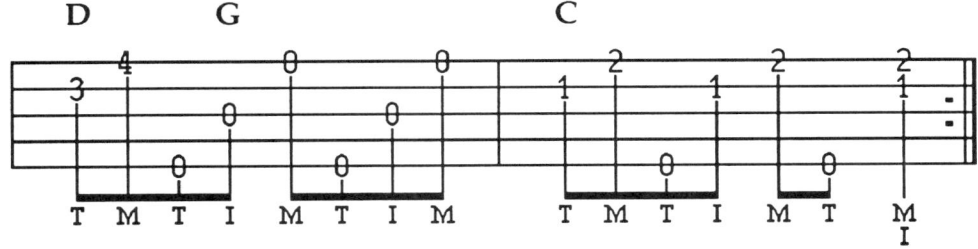

THE REST

A <u>Rest</u> is a period of silence. Rests are seldom seen in banjo tab because of the nature of the three-finger style - where other instruments may have a rest, the three-finger banjoist usually plays fill notes. However, there will often be a rest before the ending in most songs. It should be understood that even though no note is played, the rest is still counted - it takes up part of the measure and is assigned a beat, part of a beat, or several beats, depending upon what kind of rest it is.

Below is an <u>Eighth Rest</u>. Like an eighth note, it receives one half of a count.

EIGHTH REST

This is a <u>Quarter Rest</u>. Like a quarter note, it receives one count.

QUARTER REST

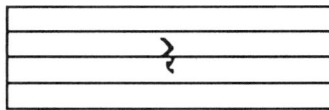

This is a <u>Half Rest</u>. It receives two counts, or the same amount of time as two quarter notes.

HALF REST

The various rests can be combined within the measure to denote a period of silence of any duration. For instance, a *Half Rest* followed by a *Quarter Rest* denotes three beats of silence. A *Quarter Rest* followed by an *Eighth Rest* denotes one and a half beats of silence.

ENDINGS

Usually and <u>Ending</u> or <u>Tag</u> will be played after the last melody note of a tune. Several standard endings follow. Learn these endings and begin using one after every song you play.

The last note of the song is included with each tag to show how long to rest between the end of the tune and the tag.

The brush ending below is the simplest tag ending. Just strum an open **G** chord. *Br* represents the brushing of the strings in the tab.

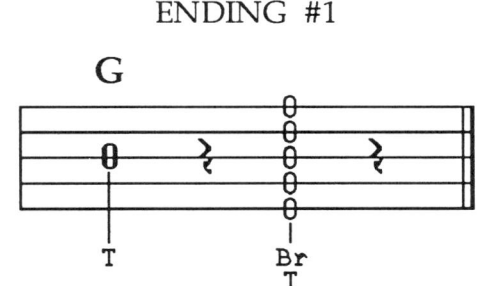

When playing ending #2 below, omit the tag lick that usually appears in the last measure of a tune.

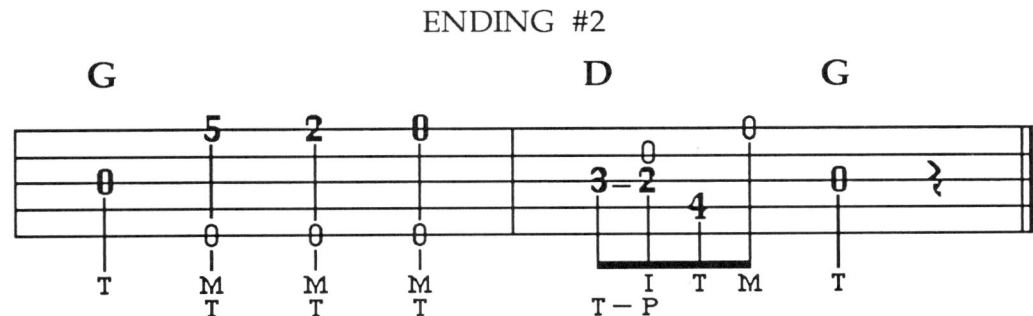

Often when playing the following ending, the last melody note (∗) of the song is omitted. The **D** chord is also optional (the rhythm could stay on **G**).

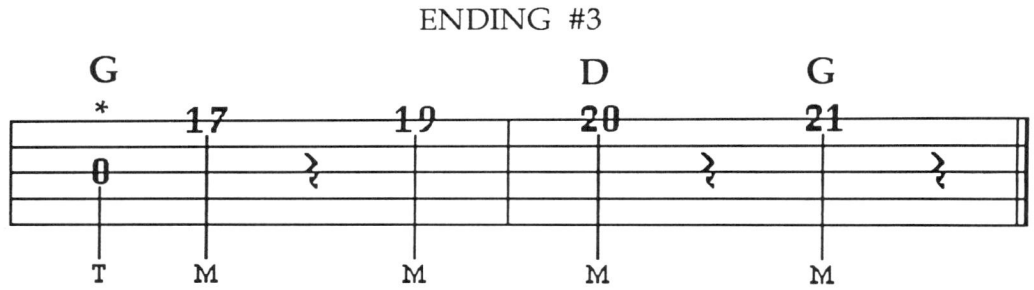

ENDING #4

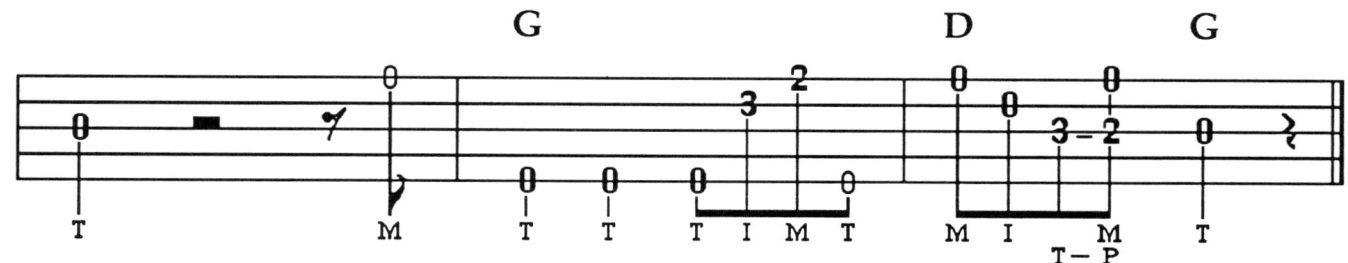

ENDING #5

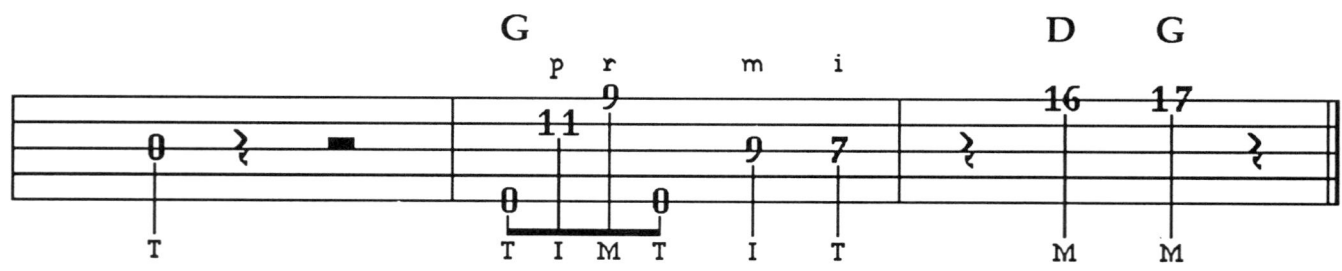

The preceding ending is known as the *Shave and a Haircut* tag. Below is another variation of this popular ending.

ENDING #6

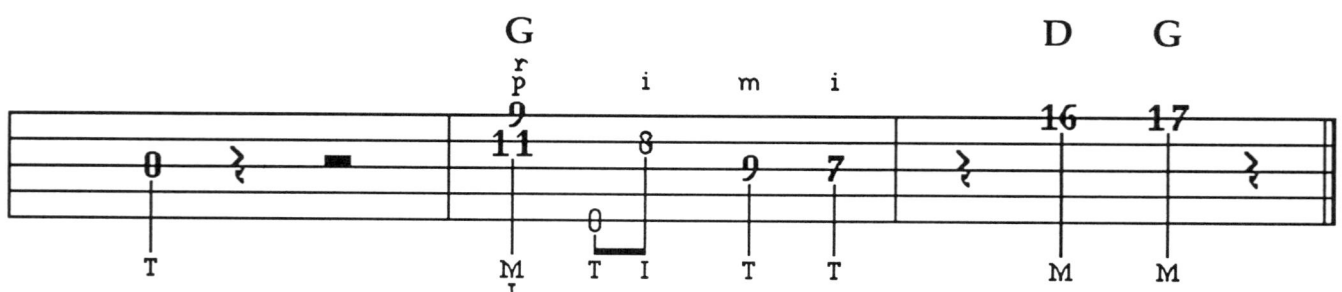

ENDING #7

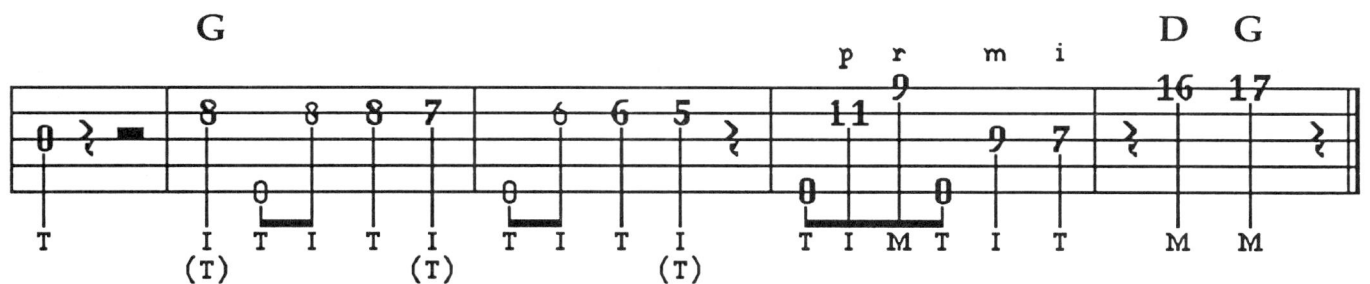

ENDING #8

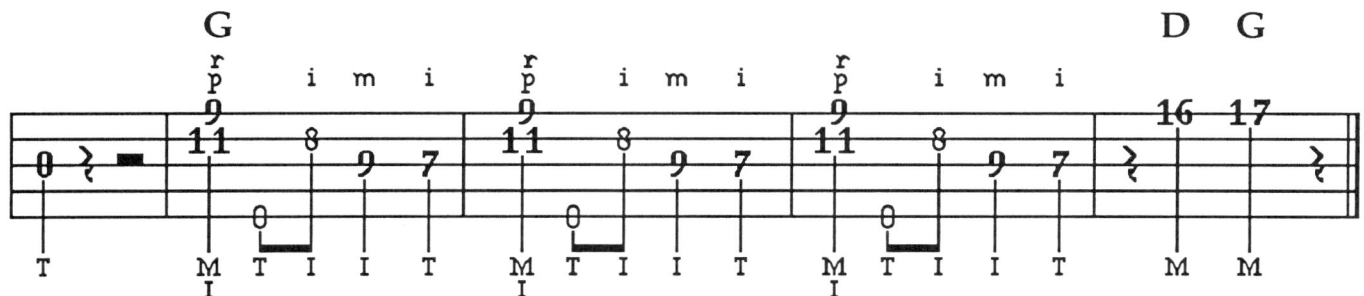

The next ending uses the Alternating Middle Roll to descend a chord scale.

ENDING #9

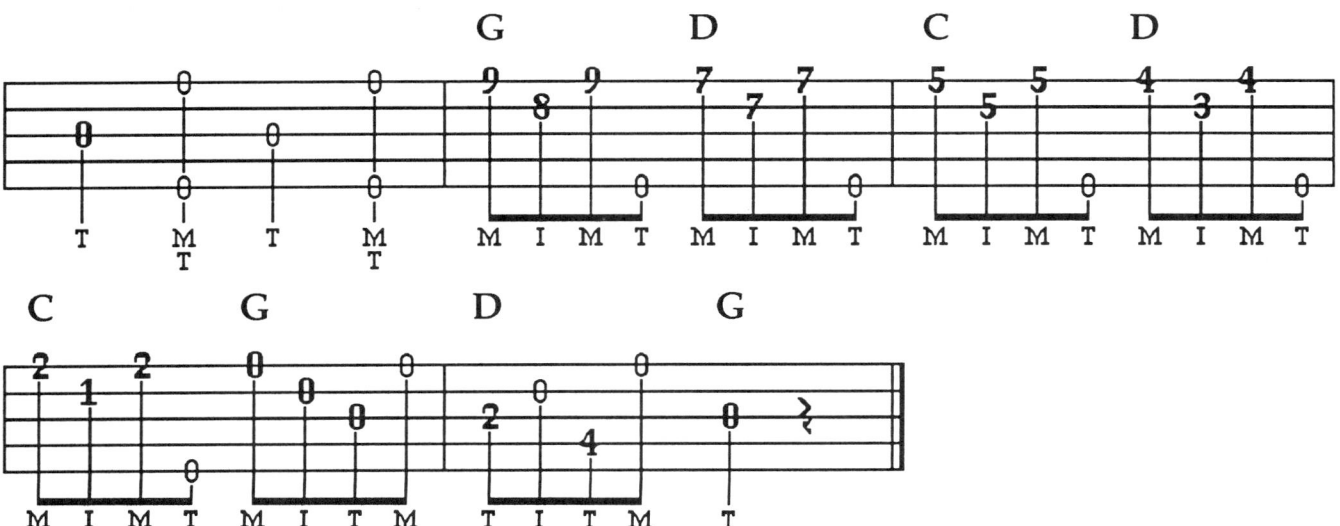

NOTES:

SONG SECTION

The basic rolls and first position chords taught in this book are the ones needed to play most songs in traditional Bluegrass style. Before going on, review everything previously learned. If you are having trouble playing any of the rolls or chords, go back and practice the songs and exercises that focus on those rolls or chords. If everything can be played smoothly but not as fast as you would like, do not learn anything new for a while - concentrate on a few of your favorite songs. Play these few every day until you are satisfied with your speed. Remember, speed is not that important at this point. Be patient. The more experience you have, the faster you will be able to play. Do not get frustrated about your lack of speed. It is better to concentrate on playing with clarity and good timing. Eventually, the speed will take care of itself.

Having learned some basic rolls and chords, the next step is to learn to combine these elements fluently in any order. The melody and chord progression of a song dictate what patterns will work in a given situation. Usually there are dozens of possibilities for any given melody fragment. Some of these left and right-hand combinations (also known as *licks*) have become more popular than others and comprise the working vocabulary of bluegrass banjo players. For example, almost every banjoist knows and frequently uses the *Tag Lick*. There are many other licks, several of which you have already used in the arrangements you have learned in this book. It is important to recognize these licks and be able to play them independently of the songs that they appear in. This is one of the first steps to playing *by ear* (the ability to listen to a song and devise your own arrangement unaided by tablature or instruction).

As you learn the following arrangements, look for the individual licks and recognize the ones you have played before in other songs. Start looking at the song as a series of licks or phrases instead of a long succession of single notes with no recognizable patterns. Also notice the chord progression and note which licks go with which chords. Really LISTEN to the accompanying tape before learning the tab. See if you can figure out parts of the song without looking at the tablature first. Good Luck!

WHOA MULE, WHOA

Traditional Arranged by Jack Hatfield

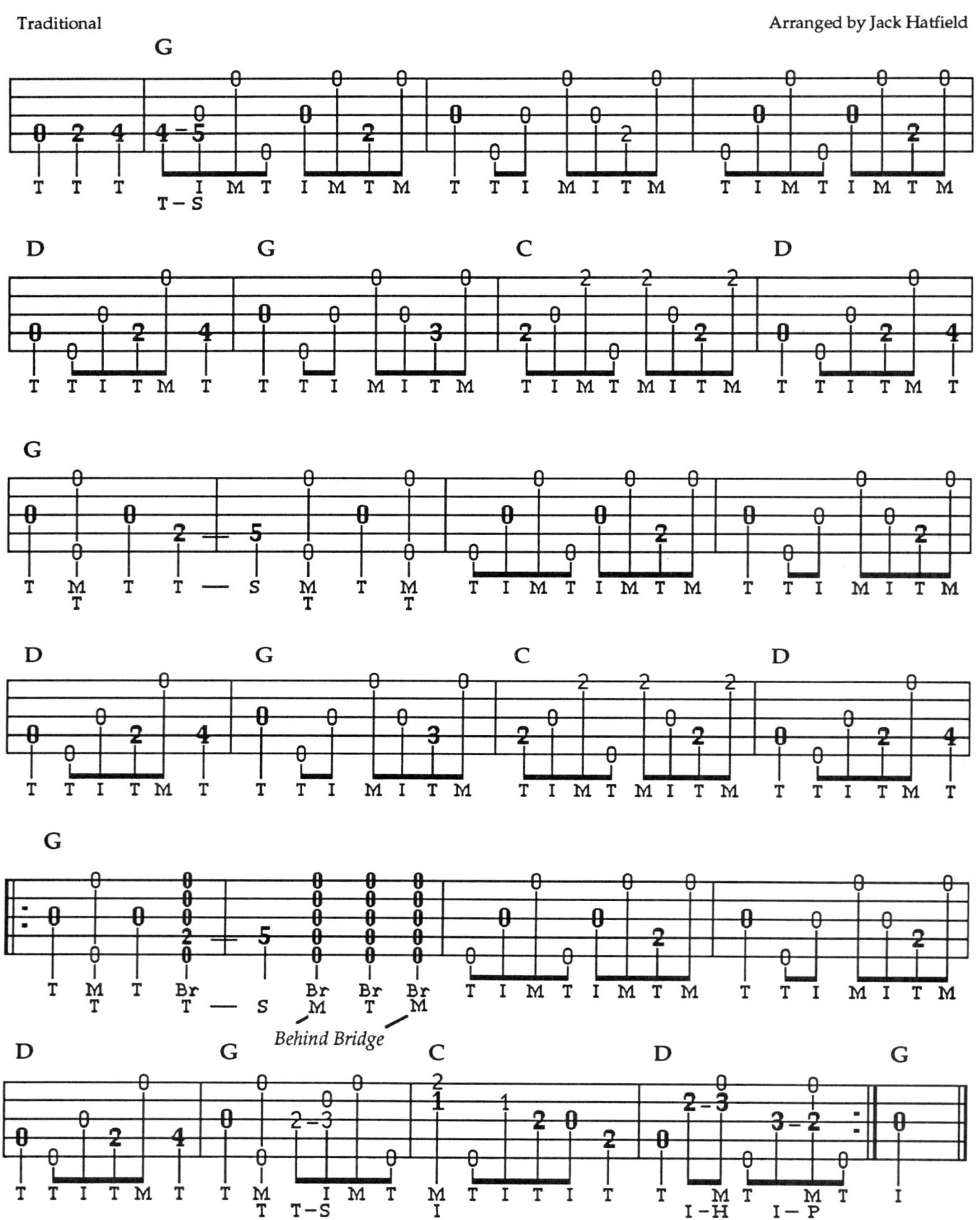

Hatfield Music
P.O. Box 6263
Knoxville, TN 37914

JOHN HARDY

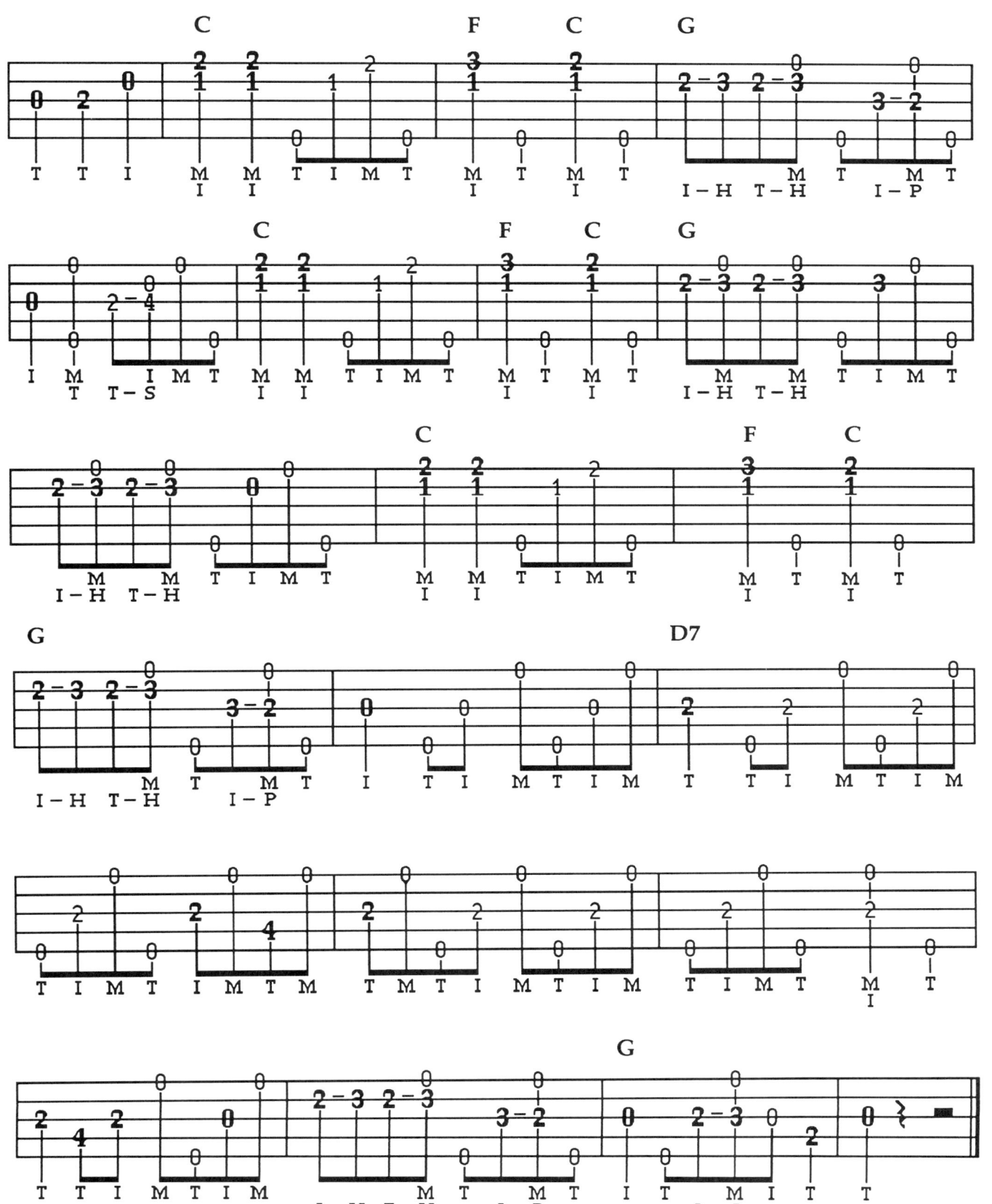

DOWN YONDER

Traditional　　　　　　　　　　　　　　　　　　　　　　　　Arranged by Jack Hatfield

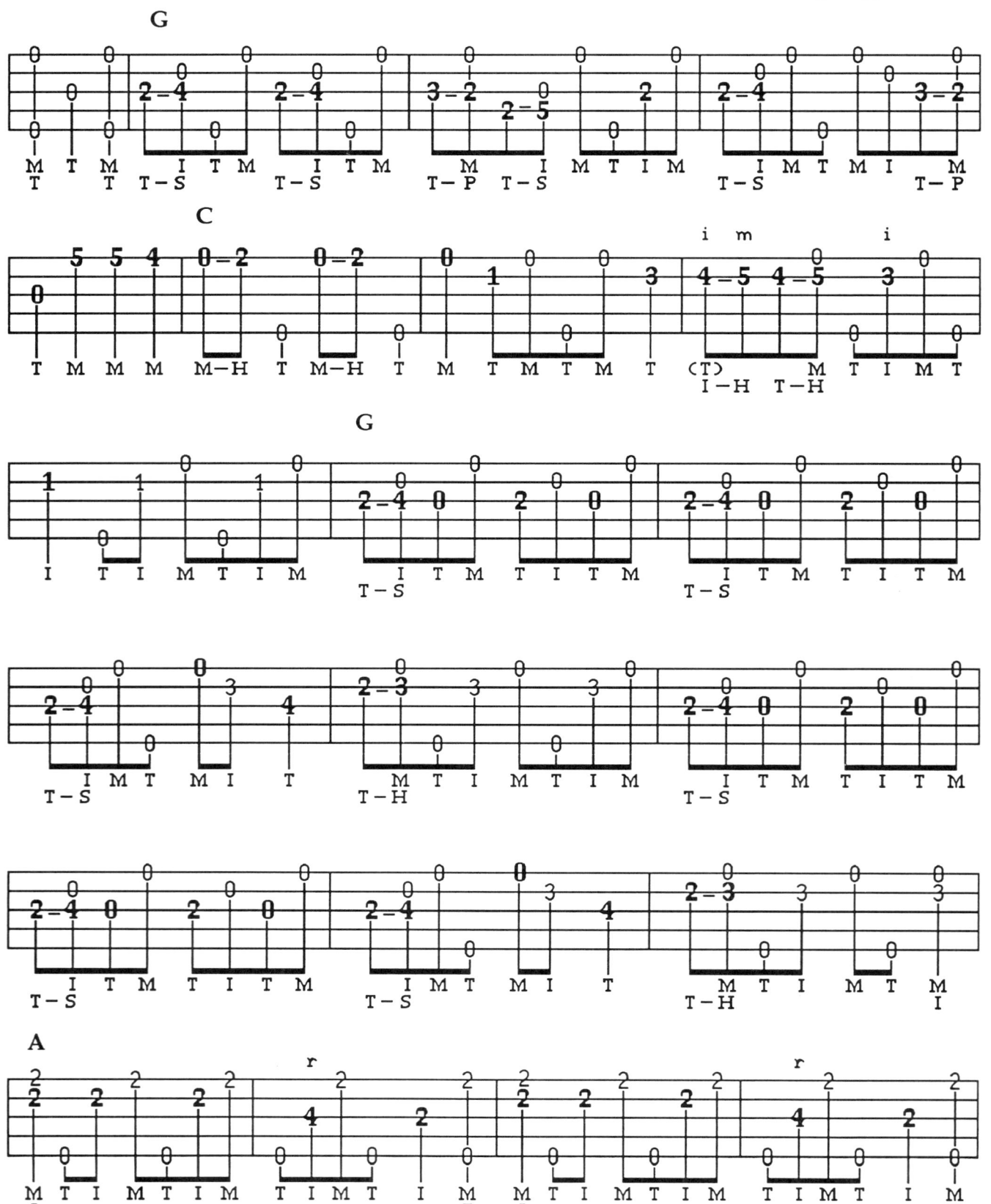

DOWN YONDER
(Continued)

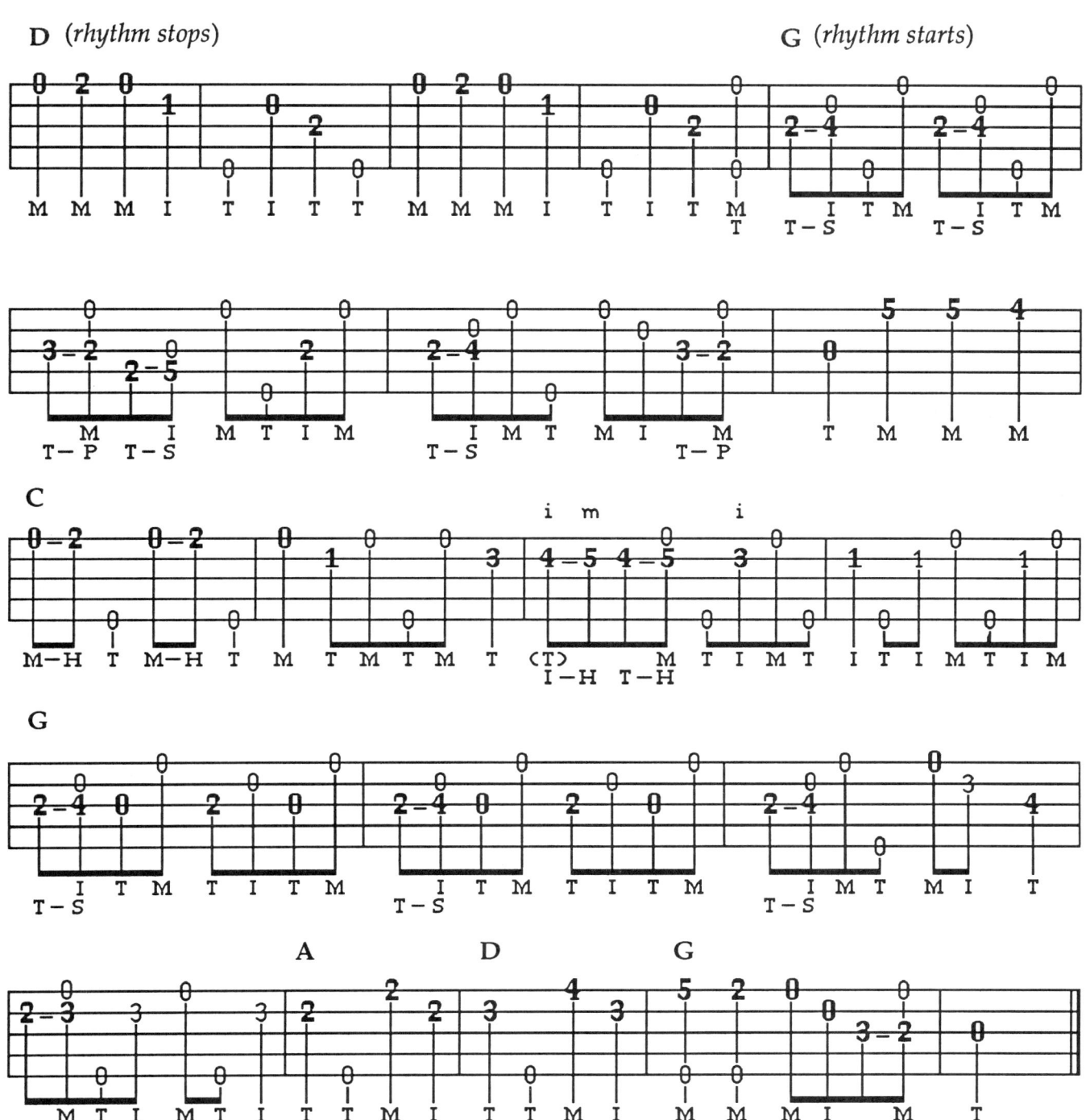

Hatfield Music
P.O. Box 6263
Knoxville, TN 37914

ROCKY TOP

Boudleaux and Felice Bryant

Arranged by Jack Hatfield

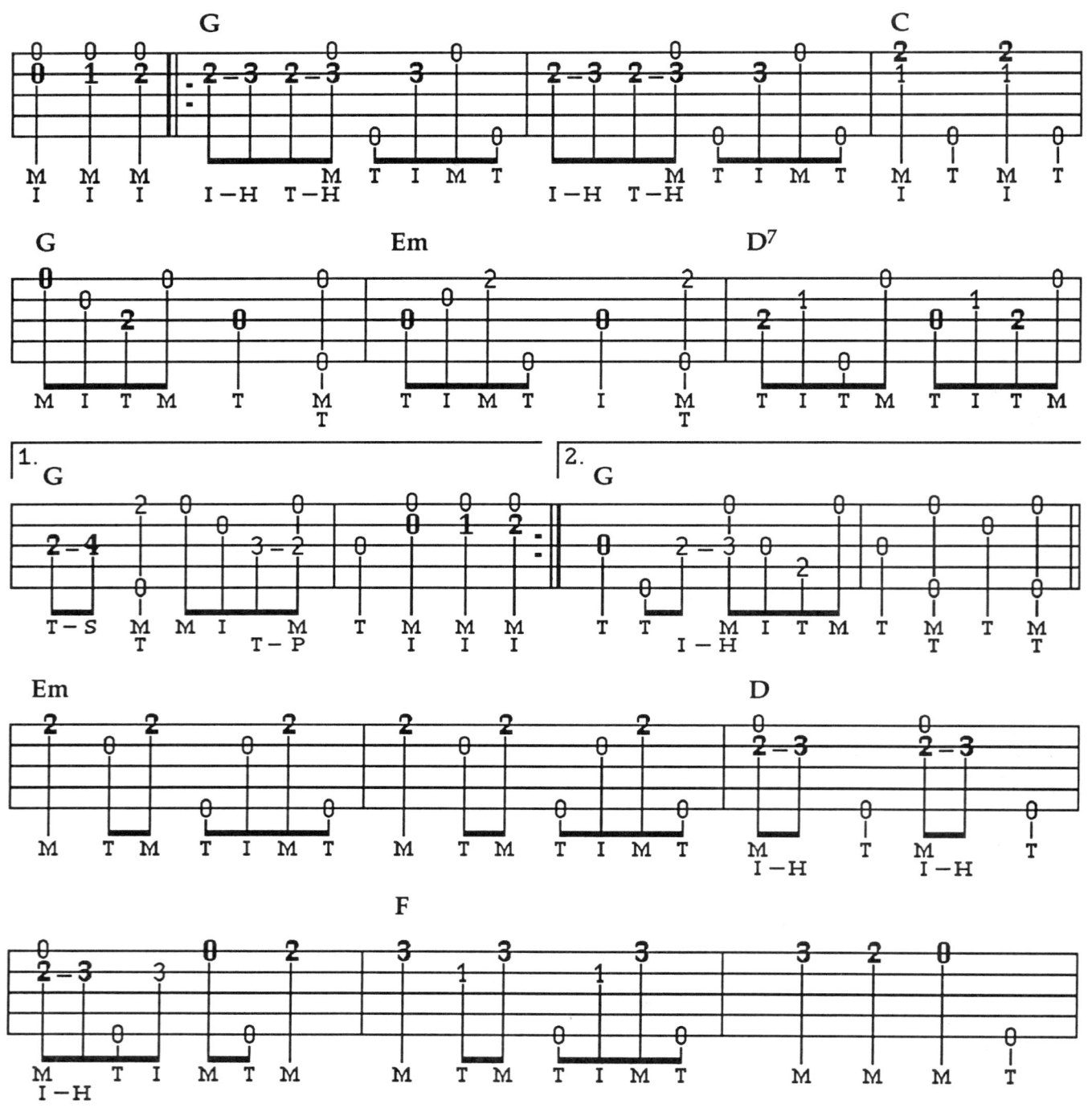

© 1967 House of Bryant Publications
P. O. Box 570 Gatlinburg, TN 37738
International Copyright Secured
All Rights Reserved

ROCKY TOP
(Continued)

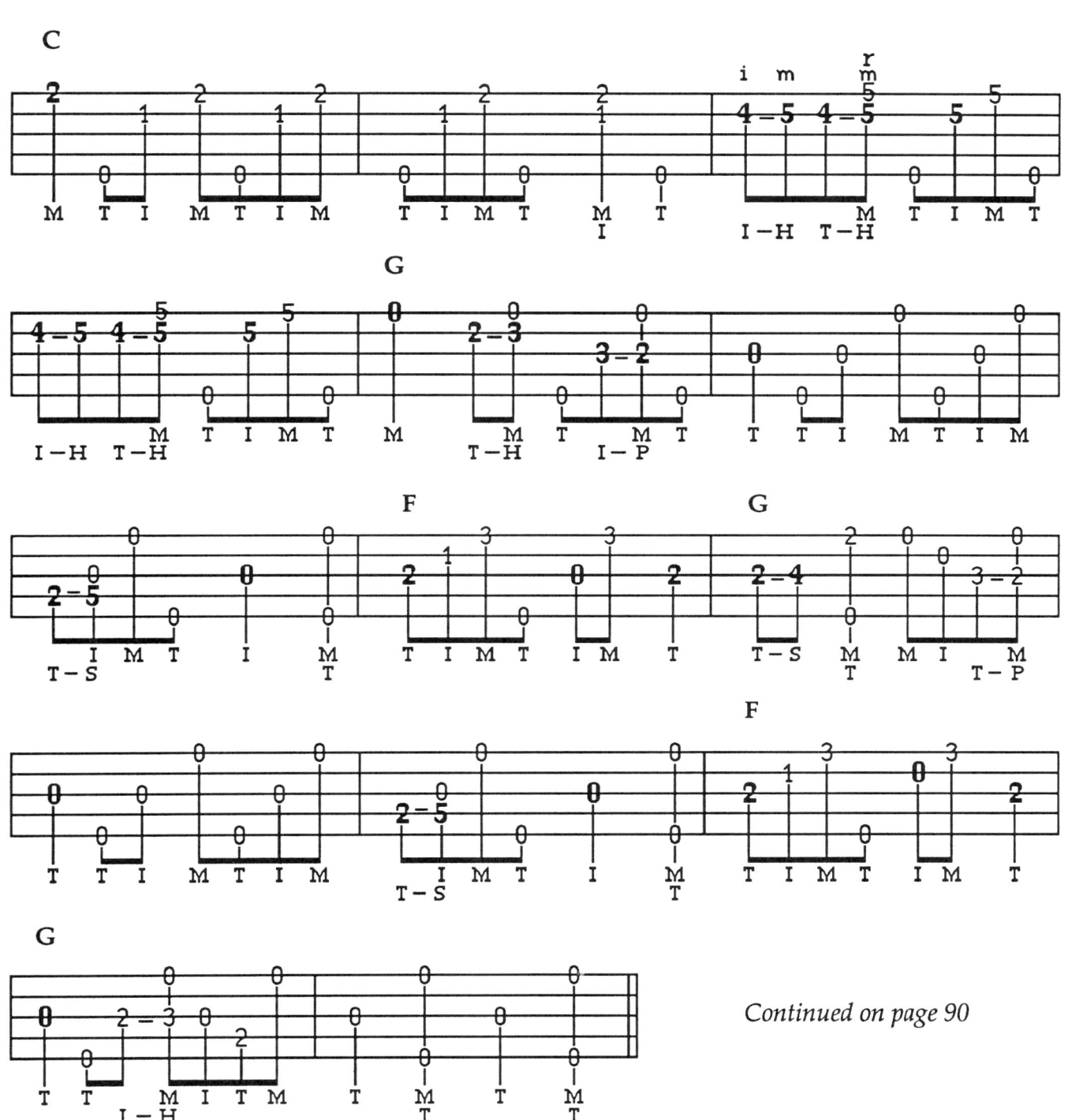

Continued on page 90

Hatfield Music
P.O. Box 6263
Knoxville, TN 37914

ROCKY TOP
(Final Ending)

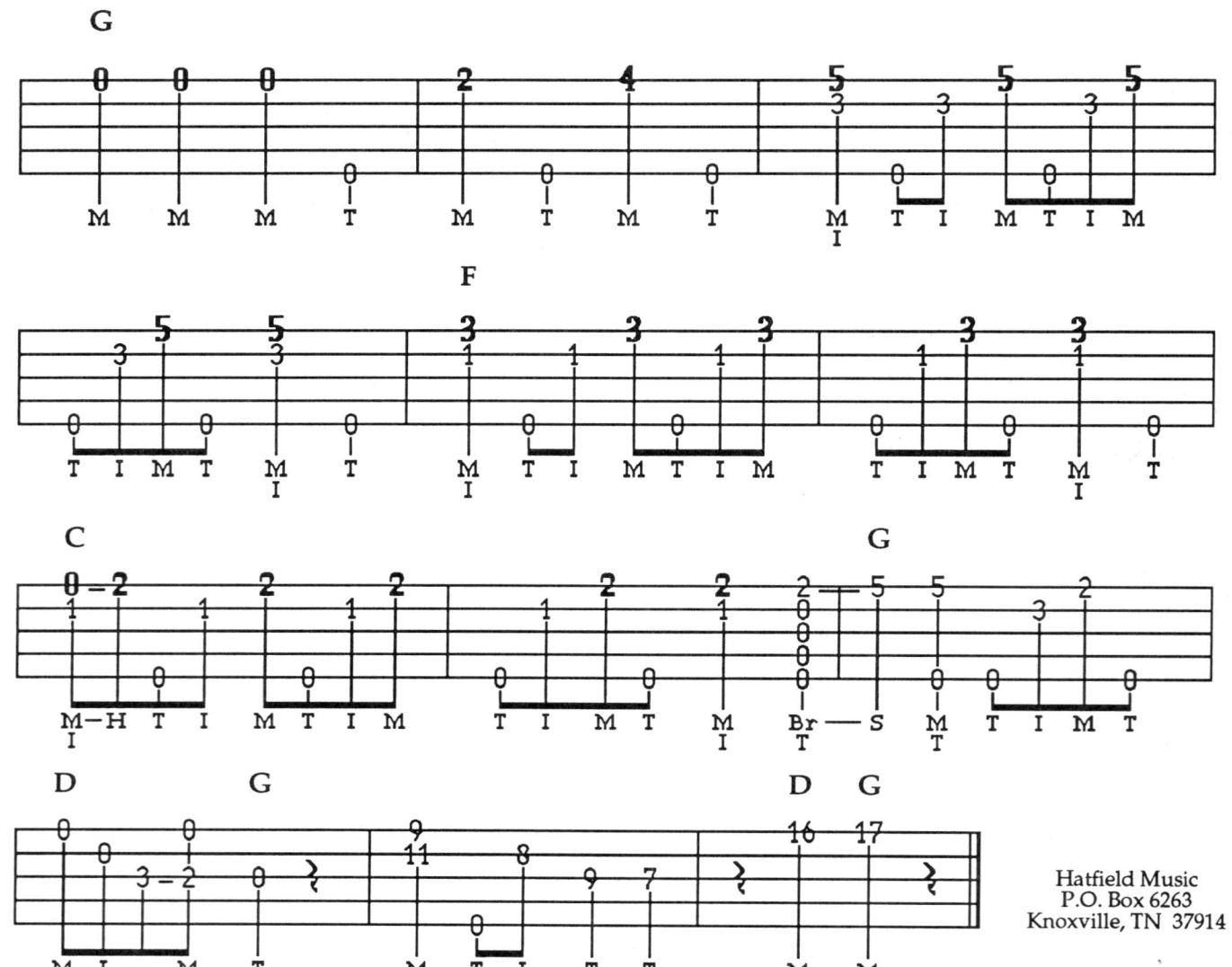

Hatfield Music
P.O. Box 6263
Knoxville, TN 37914

INDEX OF SONGS

BANKS OF THE OHIO	53
BOIL THEM CABBAGE	28
BURY ME BENEATH THE WILLOW	57
CRIPPLE CREEK	60
COMING 'ROUND THE MOUNTAIN	51
D BANJO BOOGIE	72
DOWN YONDER	86
GOOD NIGHT LADIES - Part One	23
GOOD NIGHT LADIES - Part Two	27
HANDSOME MOLLY	67
HOME SWEET HOME	49
JOHN HARDY	85
JOHN HENRY	69
LITTLE MAGGIE	74
MAKE ME A PALLET ON YOUR FLOOR	75
MOUNTAIN DEW	55
MY OLD KENTUCKY HOME - Verse	42
MY OLD KENTUCKY HOME - Chorus	45
OLD JOE CLARK	66
OLD TIME RELIGION	63
ROCKY TOP	88
SAIL AWAY LADIES	73
SOURWOOD MOUNTAIN	36
TOM DOOLEY	30
TRAIN '45	65
TWO DOLLAR BILL	39
WHOA MULE, WHOA	84
WILL THE CIRCLE BE UNBROKEN	71

A listing of other books, tablatures and recordings by Jack Hatfield is presented on the following page to help further your pursuit of three-finger style banjo playing.

Other Publications by Jack Hatfield

BLUEGRASS BANJO METHOD - BOOK TWO
Takes up where BBM-1 leaves off. Covers intermediate level topics such as: Playing in 3/4 time, Playing Up the Neck, Playing in Different Keys and Learning the Fingerboard. Features a systematic approach to learning all major, minor, and seventh chords on the entire fingerboard by memorizing nine simple formations. Includes up-the-neck solos to many songs whichwere presented in Book One. Includes demo C.D. or cassette tape with banjo on one channel and rhythm instruments on the other so you can "play along with the band".

RHYTHM TRAX™ Practice Recordings
Guitar, mandolin and bass play rhythm to the most popular bluegrass instrumentals while you play lead. Ten tunes on each tape or C.D; slow on one side, fast on the other. Companion books available for banjo, guitar, fiddle and mandolin (See TUNES™ ad below). Send S.A.S.E. for listing of tunes. Four recordings available:

BANJO TUNES - VOLUME 1
BANJO TUNES - VOLUME 2
FIDDLE TUNES - VOLUME 1
FIDDLE TUNES - VOLUME 2

Send long S.A.S.E. with 2 oz postage or see website for list of song titles.

TUNES™ Books
Each book contains tablature and/or musical notation for ten popular bluegrass instrumentals. Coincides with the RHYTHM TRAX™ practice recordings listed above. Send S.A.S.E. for listing of tunes.

BANJO TUNES - VOLUME 1
BANJO TUNES - VOLUME 2
FIDDLE TUNES - VOLUME 1
FIDDLE TUNES - VOLUME 2
FIDDLE TUNES FOR BANJO - VOLUME 1
FIDDLE TUNES FOR BANJO - VOLUME 2
FIDDLE TUNES FOR MANDOLIN - VOLUME 1
FIDDLE TUNES FOR MANDOLIN - VOLUME 2
FIDDLE TUNES FOR GUITAR - VOLUME 1
FIDDLE TUNES FOR GUITAR - VOLUME 2

JACK HATFIELD BANJO TABLATURE ARRANGEMENTS
Hundreds of arrangements. Beginner to advanced, in Scruggs, melodic, and single-string styles. Includes 56 note-for-note Earl Scruggs transcriptions, many with backup. Also, Jack Hatfield's *Beginner's Corner Collections*, *Gospel Collection*, and *Christmas Collection*, all with slow/fast recording. Send long S.A.S.E. for list.

YOU CAN TEACH YOURSELF® BANJO BY EAR
YOU CAN TEACH YOURSELF® MANDOLIN BY EAR
Learnhow to figure out chord progressions and melodies by ear, "fake" a solo, create a melody-oriented solo, and use licks to fake a solo or embellish the melody-oriented solo. Includes demo C.D. - Mel Bay Publications, Inc.

ROUNDER OLD-TIME MUSIC FOR BANJO ®
Twenty-three arrangements in various old-time and three-finger bluegrass styles, intermediate to advanced levels. Coincides with Rounder records compact disc of the same name. Mel Bay publications, Inc.

OLD-TIME GOSPEL BANJO SONGBOOK®
Banjo tablature, musical notation, and lyrics to thirty of the most-loved gospel songs, arranged from beginner to advanced, including up-the-neck solos. Includes compact disc demo recording. Mel Bay publications, Inc.

HOW TO PLAY BY EAR - A Guide for Musicians, Songwriters, and Composers.
Written for any musician on any instrument. Great for songwriters and those who are dependent on notation or tab. Explains number system, scales, chord construction, identifying chords by ear, song form, probabilities, and a step-by-step procedure that simplifies the trial-and-error process. Many ear training exercises on recording.

HATFIELD MUSIC CATALOG
In-depth descriptions and prices of the Hatfield Music publications listed above plus: Books by other authors, word books, accessories, instructional videos, T-shirts, and practice aids. Send long S.A.S.E. with 2 oz. postage.

HATFIELD MUSIC P.O. BOX 6263 KNOXVILLE, TN 37914 1-800-426-8744
Website: http://www.hatfieldmusic.com Email: hatfield@tdsnet.com